EVERYTHING I LEARNED ABOUT LIFE, I LEARNED IN DANCE CLASS

EVERYTHING I LEARNED ABOUT LIFE, I LEARNED IN DANCE CLASS

ABBY LEE MILLER
with Peter Economy

wm

WILLIAM MORROW

An Imprint of HarperCollinsPublishers

The names of certain individuals have been changed to protect their privacy.

HarperCollins books may be purchased for educational, business, or sales pro-
motional use. For information please e-mail the Special Markets Department
at SPsales@harpercollins.com.

FIRST EDITION

Dancer silhouette images © by Chris Hoye
Designed by Lisa Stokes

Library of Congress Cataloging-in-Publication Data has been applied for.

ISBN 978-0-06-230481-0

14 15 16 17 18   OV/RRD   10 9 8 7 6 5 4 3 2 1

This book is dedicated in loving memory to Maryen L. Miller,
George L. Miller, and Broadway Baby too

CONTENTS

I wish you could all dance in my shoes for a day—then you would know the real Abby Lee!

Believe it or not, Abby and I are a lot alike. *How,* you ask? Well, we both decided at a very young age exactly what we wanted to do with our lives. Abby just knew she would be a famous dance teacher, and nothing was going to get in her way—especially not people telling her that she wasn't good enough or wasn't old enough. Who can say that they have been an award-winning choreographer since the age of fourteen? Abby Lee Miller, that's who! Her résumé, longer than long, shows just how many students she has successfully prepared to achieve their goals. Abby will go to the end of the earth to help "her kids" fulfill their dreams while living her own dream at the very same time.

Abby has prepared me completely for the professional

dance world—and I'm only eleven years old! She is the best at what she does. Abby has taught me proper technique, the value of hard work, and how to learn detailed choreography quickly. She taught me how to really *hear* the music and then present the story of my dance routine with my emotions. I don't dance like no one is watching; I dance like *everyone* is watching!

Dancers always ask me how I learned to leap so high or turn so fast. Is it practice or talent or technique? It is hard to explain how Abby not only teaches her students the *how* but also the *why, what, where,* and the *when.* This is what makes Abby *so* good at what she does—every breath, every note, every movement, every glance—they all create a story. Every single thing matters.

And yes, everyone is replaceable. Because if you aren't willing to give 100 percent, then why should your dance teacher? After my performances, she is the first person I look for. She tells me what was good and what I still need to work on. I'm not afraid of her critique; I need to hear the truth. Her expertise is exactly what has made me the dancer that I am today.

Because of Abby, I am already living my dream. I cannot wait to see what tomorrow brings, and for that I'm forever grateful to my fairy godmother, Abby Lee Miller!

You will learn so much more about Abby in this book, and I know you will fall in love with her too!

MADDIE ZIEGLER

EVERYTHING I LEARNED ABOUT LIFE, I LEARNED IN DANCE CLASS

OVERTURE

IS IT EVER GOING to be good enough for me?

Probably not.

I'm Abby Lee Miller, creative director, chief choreographer, and founder of the Abby Lee Dance Company. You may know me from the hit TV shows *Dance Moms* and *Abby's Ultimate Dance Competition*, where I showcase my passionate, unapologetic, and tough-as-nails teaching style. Some people think I'm too hard on my students, but no one argues with my results. My kids shine, my teams win, and my alumni go on to Broadway careers. I'm not going to apologize for helping kids achieve more than they ever dreamed possible. My dreams for them are often bigger than the dreams they have for themselves. The kids I take under my wing know they're not in for an easy ride. That makes some moms a little uncomfortable, and I often get an earful. But that's okay; I can take it. I've been called a lot worse by a lot better people.

Say what you want about me, I get the job done. That job is helping young people excel and get the most out of life—whatever aspirations or ambitions they have. I don't believe in the word *impossible*. I make stars; it's what I do. If you want to know how to help your child be the favorite or shine in the spotlight, read on. My advice is not for the weak or meek or even the ambivalent. You have to want it 110 percent. You have to eat, sleep, and breathe your passion, and fight for perfection every step of the way. I expect a lot from the children I work with. I don't settle for second best, nor do I allow *them* to settle for less. If you can't cut the mustard, you're gone.

If you watch my shows, you know there are a lot of "Abbyisms." That's what I call my philosophies on hard work, competition, and life in general. All my kids know them like the backs of their hands and they take them to heart. They know it's not just talk—it's the rules we live by. From figuring out what you do well, to applying yourself, to laying the groundwork for an exciting career, my rules can help you achieve optimal results in the dance studio and beyond. So many parents and kids have asked me to share them that I decided it was high time I explained how and why my methods work. Why not write it all down in the form of a book? Of course I'll dish the dirt that my *Dance Moms* fans are eager to hear, and even get some of my illustrious alums to share their success stories and what was it like to get their first big break (starring roles on Broadway and in television and films). Right out of (dancing) school? You bet! Many have gone from living in the Pitts to a house in the Hamptons!

So what makes me an expert?

Dancing and competing are in my blood. I've been teaching dance, choreographing, and winning competitions since I was fourteen years old. I was there in the beginning when dance competitions were just starting, and I jumped on board. I founded the Abby Lee Dance Company in 1980 with the sole goal of creating champions, and I've been doing so ever since. I know that parents want the very best for their children, and I'm here to tell you that training starts as early as a toddler can walk into the studio. Every step in a child's life is an opportunity to learn, to grow, and to achieve.

My rules apply to any activity, not just dance—from the soccer field to the swimming pool to the classroom. I don't believe in coddling kids. Coddling is not loving; it's indulging and overprotecting. A loving parent knows when and where to be firm and how to encourage and coax the best out of her kid. Buffer your child from the real world and she won't learn how to deal with it. Allow your child to be lazy, bratty, or a crybaby, and you'll wind up with an irresponsible, complaining, helpless adult who needs a loan or a spare room in your house for the next few years.

You've probably heard a lot of talk about "helicopter parenting"—moms and dads who hover around, trying to shield their children from failure, pain, or disappointment. Well, guess what? You're also preventing them from achieving any kind of greatness. Kids who are constantly sheltered from criticism and praised for a mediocre performance will stop working hard. Why should they have to? They're getting applause anyway. The parents' job is to raise children to survive without them—*period*. Teach a kid to stand on her own two feet—to respect her peers and her teachers and to push herself constantly to be better, stronger, and smarter—and you've done your job. Anything less than that, I consider a parenting failure.

Whenever a kid screws up, I know there's always a dance mom to blame.

I tell moms when they walk through the door of my studio for the first time that if you want someone to hold your hand, you've come to the wrong place. I expect parents to learn right along with their children, which is why you'll find "Are You Mom Enough?" quizzes in the book just for you. In case you need a quick reminder or refresher course now and then, there's "Abby's Ultimate Advice" at the end of each chapter, outlining the key steps you need to take at every age and stage of your child's development.

I always tell my students, "Save those tears for your pillow"—and I mean it. Whining, wallowing, wimping out—I don't stand for it. (Moms, that goes for you too!) If you're not prepared to give me 110 percent, there's the door. Don't let it hit your derrière on the way out.

But if you are willing to work, sacrifice, and *believe*, the sky's the limit. Some say, "Anything is possible." I say, "*Everything* is possible!"

OPENING NUMBER
Welcome to Abby's World

Who the hell is this fourteen-year-old kid
telling everyone what to do?
Abby Lee Miller—the dance teacher's daughter!

WHEN I WAS ABOUT EIGHTEEN YEARS OLD, a fortune-teller read my aura at a charity event and asked me how many kids I had.

"None," I answered truthfully.

"No—that can't be," she insisted. "I see hundreds and hundreds of children at your feet."

I thought at the time that she should probably invest in a new crystal ball—she was barking up the wrong tree. But now I realize she actually did catch a glimpse of my future, even if I couldn't see that far down the road at the time. Yes, I have hundreds and hundreds of kids in my life and in my dance studio. And yes, in a lot of ways, I am a mom to each and every one of them. But did I ever see this coming? No way. I always tell my students that I dream bigger for them than I do for myself, and that's the truth.

I never wanted to be a dancer or a dance teacher. I just knew what I *didn't* want to be. Even though my parents gave me all sorts of lessons, there was no way I was going to be a professional ski instructor, a career Girl Scout, a Roller Derby girl, or an Olympic ice-skater. I also knew—despite the fact that my mother was a dancer and owned several dance studios—that I did *not* want to be a performer. That's hard work! You have to be *on* all the time. Your hair has to be done, your nails polished, your body in peak condition. But I always wanted to be on the creative side, and I always wanted to be my own boss.

My mother, Maryen Lorrain Miller (maiden name McKay), was a fifty-year member of Dance Masters of America, and she owned seven dance studios in Miami before she married my dad and had me. I was born in 1965. Life was grand, business was booming, and women wore high heels with their aprons. They had a martini waiting for their husbands when they got home from work. After I was born, my mom was going to become one of these "domestic engineers." Maryen was intent on staying at home with her brand-new bundle of joy.

That's me: Abby Lee.

I was named after the most beautiful girl my dad ever dated (needless to say, Abigale was *not* my mother's name). My mom and dad were thirty-six when they got married and thirty-eight when they had me. They purchased a model home in the suburbs and joined the country club. Things were going great for a few months until my mother accidently let me roll out of my infant carrier and fall off the dining room table. At that moment it occurred to her that maybe she wasn't cut out for this stay-at-home mom business after all.

Truthfully, she missed her former life: "Swing and sway with Maryen McKay." She taught hundreds of children in the South Florida area, from the Southwest section, to Perine, Coral Gables, the Northwest section, North Miami Beach, and South Beach. She pretty much had every square inch of the Miami area covered. Television shows, commercials, and movies were filmed in this sun-drenched, pink-and-turquoise celebrity vacation spot. She turned her students into professional, paid dancers— performing behind Dean Martin and Sammy Davis Jr. in the glamorous supper clubs at the Fontainebleau Hotel. My mom shopped at the upscale boutiques on Lincoln Road and drove a big Cadillac convertible. With her business thriving and more opportunities coming her way, she was too busy to think about a husband and family. The thing that changed her mind was her mother dying of what they thought to be breast cancer.

My parents were born on the same street in a Pittsburgh neighborhood known as Greenfield. They flirted as preteens and dated on and off in high school. Then Maryen McKay moved along with her mom and dad to Miami, Florida. She supported her parents with money earned by teaching children how to dance. She created a livelihood out of her passion. Miss McKay was creative, knowledgeable, and very kind. Mrs. McKay managed the books, the costumes, and the inner workings of the studios. The two were as thick as thieves. Without her mom, my mom was lost.

After the war was over, George L. "Salty" Miller would come all the way to South Florida, take my mom out on one date, then spend the rest of his time at Gulfstream Park racetrack. I'm convinced that's where he left my inheritance! Back to the story: my dad came down to be at my mother's side during this very difficult time—he brought a note that his own mother had left for him when she passed away a few months earlier. The note was a wish list for each of her six children. Her wish for Salty was that he would marry that nice Maryen McKay in Florida!

So the event was planned and there was a spectacular wedding in Pittsburgh, plus another celebration down south. For some time, my mother commuted back and forth. If Dad thought she was going to sit on the front porch with rollers in her hair gossiping with the neighbors, he had another think coming! Her self-imposed retirement only lasted a few months (thanks to my falling off the dining room table). She then opened her first studio in Pittsburgh, in the little steel town where they both grew up.

My dad was a yardmaster for the Monongahela Connecting Railroad in conjunction with the J&L Steel Corporation. He came home from work around 3:00 P.M. and my mom headed to her dance studio half an hour later. His job provided lots of security and excellent benefits. My friends got stocks and bonds for their birthdays. I got the Barbie Dream House, the boat, and the plane. Mom's dance business took care of the trips to Disney World, my shoe addiction, and all the equipment needed for my ridiculous number of activities.

I quickly became Daddy's Little Girl. He was going to make sure I had everything he never had. He made my ponytails so tight my eyebrows rose up an inch higher. He dropped me off at Brownies, then picked me up from CCD (religion classes at the local Catholic church). The poor guy sat through countless painful roller-skating, ice-skating, and clarinet lessons. He broke down and bought the skis, and then even joined me on the slopes. He was probably most excited purchasing my cute spikes for Junior Golf at the club. From Memorial Day to Labor Day, Mr. Miller ran the swim team program at our pool. He did it all; he even had to take me to the Mother-Daughter Talk at school.

So I was well-rounded: good at everything yet great at nothing. Did I dance? Yes, of course I did. But I went once a week with my friends from the neighborhood. My mom didn't play favorites. She was kind and giving and wonderful to everyone who graced her presence. She never pushed me, nor put me front and center. She knew too many instructors who ruined their businesses by fea-turing their own daughters in every number. This turns people off! I didn't even get to go down the mat first in tumbling class. Jeez!

Despite all the exercise, I was sick a lot as a kid (maybe because my dad smoked unfiltered Camels? Hello, people!). I spent a lot of time at my pediatrician's office, and I'll never forget him: Dr. Mendel Silverman. I loved him, and I loved going once a week to get my allergy shot (I'm not a freak, the shot hurt like hell!). I loved Little's Super Shoe Store (I still shop there regularly), and the 31 Flavors ice cream place we visited often, and most of all S. W. Randall's Toyes and Giftes (yes—that's the way they spell it!). I knew I was a creative person way back then because all the grandiose traditional dollhouses on display did nothing for me. I had to have my dad get some guy at work to build me an A-frame ski house with Plexiglas see-through floors and a spiral staircase. I had to decorate it and furnish it to my exact taste and specifications. Control freak? Maybe. But it was the most amazing dollhouse anyone had ever seen.

By middle school, I was accompanying my mom to regional dance conferences and seminars. She liked having company, and I liked getting out of school, socializing, and of course stopping on the way home to eat. We loved visiting the Cicci's Dance Supply factory, a family-owned business that produces costumes for dance studios across the nation. I had the gift of gab, so I could easily find out how they made everything so beautifully. I would talk to the seamstresses, watch them use a ruffling machine, and pick up scraps to make headpieces or Barbie clothes. This was probably the moment when my passion for designing costumes was born.

These day trips grew into holiday study trips and eventually summers attending back-to-back national dance conventions. I loved seeing different dance styles demonstrated by master instructors across the United States. Their innovative new takes on classic technique inspired me. When I was just thirteen, looking through the mail on the kitchen table for department store sale flyers, I saw that a dance competition was coming to my town.

"Mom," I asked, "how exactly does that work—and what can I win?" Not knowing much about these new-fangled types of dance competitions, my mom thought it was ridiculous for students to pay to compete. She was used to her students *being paid* to perform. Well, it turned out that Pittsburgh is a lot different from Miami Beach! Paying to be in dance competitions was our only way to get onstage and perform. I coerced my three girlfriends to enter into this adventure with me, and we were off and running—or should I say off and rolling! I choreographed my first trio—using skateboards. One girl was in red, another in blue, and the third in green. The competition was called Summer Dance Festival, and *we won first place*! We thought this was an amazing accomplishment. The prize was just a dinky little trophy, but the sense of pride was like no other!

That fall, when everyone was doing back-to-school shopping, I couldn't have cared less about clothes, and classes, and football games. I was totally consumed with going back to dancing school and my plans for the future. I had convinced my mom to let me start my very own dance company competition team. Obviously, her best students—the teenagers from fifteen to eighteen—were off-limits; they weren't going to listen to some little kid who was younger than them. But my mom agreed to let me hold auditions for her students between the ages of seven and twelve—coincidentally, the exact age range of the cast of *Dance Moms* when it began. The original Abby Lee Dance Company was founded in September of 1980, when I was just fourteen years old!

Suddenly I found myself in charge of all these other people's children and their futures in dance. I was telling their parents what to do, where to go, even which outfit to wear. And they listened. This was a big undertaking, and I felt I had a huge responsibility to make the best dancers possible. It was at this point that I realized I had been given quite an extraordinary gift. My future was sealed, and I was eager to prove myself.

My days were filled with U.S. history and algebra. My nights were spent with history of movement and petite allegros. I might have been your average student during my typical school day, but after school, I was quickly becoming a master teacher. While my friends were looking for a future career in the guidance counselor's office,

I was proving to my colleagues that I had already found my true vocation.

The first group number I entered into the Regency Talent Competition *won first place*! It may have been another plastic trophy with a victory eagle on top, but the thrill of the win was all I needed.

One thing led to another, and the Abby Lee Dance Company became a force to be reckoned with in the dance community. Over the course of twenty years—and a *lot* of work—my competition team grew from twelve to one hundred forty-eight, and the level of dance (and drama) continues to grow and flourish. But like the roads in Pittsburgh, the road to success has been filled with plenty of potholes along the way.

I've been devastated and defamed, but I've never felt bullied. For me, it's been about proving all those people wrong. It's made me stronger, smarter, and, let's face it, superior. I've had kids solicited away from me, I've had to deal with moms far worse than the ones you've seen on TV, and my teams have had to compete in front of judges so biased that even Baryshnikov would be lucky to get a bronze. One of the lowest of lows was discovering that two of my most trusted employees couldn't cover my classes so that I could be at the hospital when my father underwent emergency brain surgery. Why was this so devastating to me? Because I found out that the reason they couldn't help me when I needed them most was that they were teaching behind my back at another studio.

But if you had asked me way back then what I thought I was going to do with my life, I would have told you, "I'm going to move to New York City and someone is going to hand over millions of dollars so I can put up a new Broadway musical." Never did I think I was going to stay in Pittsburgh, PA. Never did I imagine I would spend a million dollars of my own savings—along with a loan from S&T Bank—on a state-of-the-art dance studio in my hometown.

Yet I know that what I do now is why I was put on this earth—it's my reason for being. Do I want to do more? You betcha. I would like to design costumes that every dancer could wear. I would like to decorate homes—starting with my own! And my dream job is to sell Lear jets—after all, you only have to sell one each year! I know I can explore these and other avenues, because I'm not afraid of hard work.

And I know *everything* is possible!

When I see talented, beautiful young people just moseying through life, I want to smack their heads together and make them pay attention! Is that what you aspire to be? Lazy and dragging up the rear? The first step to success is visualizing it. Negativity is not permitted in my dance studio (well, not by the students anyway). I want you to close your eyes and see that Broadway marquee with your name blazing across it. It isn't a fantasy; it's the start of bigger and better things to come.

Dear Abby:

I was a dancer for twenty years and I know I could help the kids on our dance team do a lot better. We came in fifth place last week! Should I offer my expertise?

Butt out. I mean it sincerely. If you've done the research and selected this teacher based on her solid reputation, then let her do her job. And don't argue. If you're given a rulebook that says you need a specific brand of dance shoes, *get them!* Do not be the mom who does her own thing, because the teacher you've spent so much time selecting will then hate your kid. Even as the parent, you must learn to follow instructions. No matter what the activity is, you will both have to play the game and be part of the team. You might have seen me spar with Holly on the TV show. Sometimes she wants special treatment for her daughter Nia. Like "You have to teach her this way, you have to teach her that way." I'm Abby Lee Miller. I don't have to do anything. Holly wants to teach me how to teach? Really? Does this help her daughter Nia to do better? To do her best? Absolutely not. So my advice to you is to mind your own business . . . or open your own dance studio.

Abby

MY DAUGHTER
by Maryen Lorrain Miller

When Abby was born, her dad said, "I'm going to take over, because I'm used to children. I'm one of six, and you're one of nothing." He went on to tell me that I didn't have any brothers and sisters, nieces or nephews, and therefore, I didn't know how to take care of a baby. I thought, "Oh, boy. Okay, that's gonna suit me fine. You can do all the work, buddy!"

Abby was slow to talk. She was three before she said a word and it was "dada" of course. Little did we know that once she started talking, she would never stop. My child was always up to something: putting on shows in the backyard, turning our garage into a haunted house, throwing elaborate carnivals for muscular dystrophy research. Her active imagination kept us both on our toes.

In fifth grade, every kid in Abby's class was picked to play an instrument. All her girlfriends got the flute, so she wasn't happy when she got the clarinet. I helped her feel better when I told her that I had to play the trombone all through high school *and* I had to carry it back and forth uphill in the snow. So her dad and I went out and got the best clarinet with the fanciest case we could find. She learned how to play the clarinet (well, kinda sorta) in the school band as well as from private lessons. During the years that she was in the school band, I had never been to any of her holiday concerts because I was always working late at the dance studio. Eventually there was a concert that I was able to catch. Apparently, the principal had told the band members that the girls were not allowed to wear pantsuits at the upcoming event; they had to wear dresses. So my daughter was sitting with her group of clarinet players, in her pretty dress, up front where everyone could see her . . . with her knees wide open!!! Abby was playing away like nobody's business. I was trying to get her attention the entire time. I couldn't wave or yell during the program, so I kept clapping my hands, exaggerating the closure. I kept hoping that she would understand that I was trying to tell her to put her legs together. Shut your legs, Abby—shut your legs! My kid definitely stole the show that day.

When Abby was growing up, she was always in the backline when she danced, and she was never a soloist. I never pushed Abby to be a great dancer. I think too many dance teachers focus on their own kids, and they forget about the kids who are paying tuition. She enjoyed coming to class and had fun interacting with the other students at my studio, and she liked all of her extracurricular activities, but she never really found her niche. One day, when she was just thirteen, Abby came home and announced that she was going to quit all of her activities, even Girl Scouts. I said, "Oh, my goodness. What are you going to do?" I had no idea what this girl was up to.

She replied, "I'm going to be a choreographer."

I said, "What?!?"

And she said, "Yes, I'm going to be a choreographer."

So that same year, Abby took two of my students, who were twin siblings, and one of her close friends, and she taught them a jazz/acrobatic routine specifically for an upcoming competition in Pittsburgh. Abby entered her trio in the contest—and they won! That was it. Abby was hooked. She knew her calling was to be a choreographer and to work with children. She made the decision on her own, and it's the only thing that she ever stuck with. I am so very proud of all that she has accomplished, the unique ideas she comes up with time after time, and the many lives that she has changed. I can rest easy knowing that my only daughter is independent, successful, and happy. I just wish she'd toss some of those mothers out!

Maryen Lorrain Miller began teaching dance in Miami Beach, Florida, in 1944. Maryen built a successful reputation in Florida as an active member of every major dance organization and a friend to all. Now her great name graces the Reign Dance Productions building, as her knowledge, curriculum, and love live on in the teaching, learning, and succeeding of everyone who enters her school. In the last weeks of life, Maryen dictated her favorite stories.

Maryen Lorrain Miller, July 6, 1927–February 8, 2014

WHAT I LOOK FOR IN A DANCER

Although people think of dancers as being tall and leggy like a Rockette, Broadway performers come in all shapes and sizes, as do the dancers you see in videos or in a concert world tour. What I look for in a dancer is excellent posture; a long leg in which the length from the hip to the knee is equal to the length from the knee to the ankle; natural turnout through the hip socket; a tight, closed rib cage; flexibility in the back, legs, and shoulders; and strength in the center core.

Flaws in a dancer's body that send up a red flag: pigeon-toed feet, swayback, rounded shoulders, extended rib cage, heavy head, extended chin. A dancer wears a leotard and her hair in a bun so that a teacher can see if she has scoliosis of the spine and make sure her head is properly aligned with her shoulders and tailbone.

A dancer's foot should have a high arch, a high instep, and be capable of being hyperextended beyond its normal position. Usually the ball of the foot is wide and the heel is very narrow. That makes it difficult to buy normal street shoes, but excellent for pointe shoe fittings.

You never want anything radical like a crazy haircut or strange outlandish hair color or tattoos or piercings. If someone hiring you for a job wants you to look like that, then they'll imagine you looking like that and they'll make sure that it's done with makeup and temporary hair dye or a wig. You want to keep your options open.

You want people to be able to look at you doing many different parts.

When you have those beautiful long limbs and that fluidity in your body and the flexibility, usually you make a gorgeous dancer, but you also need the passion, the determination, the parental support, and the musicality. Sometimes a kid who has flat feet and no flexibility, and is awkward yet has the passion and the parental support, ends up being the one who makes it, when the kid who had it all threw it away.

I've seen many incredible dancers with remarkable, God-given talent walk right out the door never to dance again and their parents don't care. That makes me sick— what a waste of talent!

FIND YOUR PASSION

So where do you start? Well, it's never too early to identify where your talents lie. Some kids are born with tons of interests and hobbies while others struggle to find one. But this I promise you: everyone can be good at *something,* whether it's hitting a ball with a bat, painting a still life, or tapping your toes. The younger you are, the more you should explore different avenues. Sitting around playing video games or chatting on Facebook is not going to inspire your mind and soul (unless you aspire to be a video game designer or a social media entrepreneur!). Take a class; try something new.

Open your mind to the possibilities. And plan on working hard.

One of my alums, Allie Meixner, showed up on my doorstep when she was just three. She was cute as a button with a sparkle in her eye. Besides being absolutely gorgeous, she had that special quality that draws people in. However, she walked with the same arm and the same foot simultaneously, which was quite awkward! "Oh, boy," I thought, "this kid might be a model someday, but she is never going to be a dancer!" Allie proved me wrong. She had a passion for dance and an amazing work ethic. She wanted to succeed more than anything else in the world. That kid had to work her booty off to get to where she is today, but she never took no for an answer.

Competition is healthy—it pushes each dancer to get better and better. I think back to all the besties who were really each other's toughest competition. There were Mark and Michelle, Katie and Kacy, Semhar and Rachel, and Koree and Allie. Who's Koree? The dancer Allie should thank in her will. There were lots of pretty girls in Allie's competition group, but the one stunner was her duet partner, Koree Kurkowski. Koree had the look, the legs, and the oh-so-wonderful feet. She was strong and physical and things came easily for her. Koree also never wore the same leotard twice!

When I put her in competition for the Junior Miss Dance title, she earned first runner-up honors, but that year they allowed the winner and the runners-up in each age division to go on to compete at the National Finals. So that summer, Koree had the opportunity to travel with me to the prestigious Nationals in Anaheim, California, and experience all the fun and life lessons with the rest of my regional title winners.

That's all it took—one kid with one opportunity—to make another kid jealous, or should I be politically correct and say to "inspire" another child? Back home in Pittsburgh, Allie was on a mission to be the best. She got up before school to work out with her mom, and she made her dad drive her to the studio an extra day each week to be a class demonstrator. She added voice lessons to her schedule. Allie went on to earn the titles Petite, Junior, Teen, and Miss Dance of Pennsylvania for the Dance Masters of America, as well as the auspicious National Preteen, Teen, and Senior Miss Dance titles for Dance Educators of America.

When you look like Allie and dance like Allie, you are destined to be the leading lady! Her first professional job out of high school, after passing up a lucrative contract to work in Japan for Tokyo Disneyland, was the national tour of the musical *Contact,* playing the coveted role of Girl in the Yellow Dress.

. . . .

Dear Abby:
My daughter is jealous of another girl on her dance team.
She says she's prettier, better, and gets all the best parts and
numbers. How can I smooth things out between them?

It's not your job as a mom to get in the middle of girl fights. Learn that first of all. Second, how about a minimakeover? If the other kid is prettier, get your kid the right haircut, the highlights, and a brand-new leotard. Do whatever it takes, including private lessons. If you end up giving that studio some extra income, your kid's going to get recognized. Also, your child will become a better dancer—maybe leaving her classmate in the dust.

Abby

. . . .

START YOUNG

It's a proven fact that kids who find a passion early in life learn faster than older kids. Most children begin to dance at the age of three, or maybe as early as two and a half if they are really smart, and four if they cling to their mother's leg.

Doesn't every little girl twirl around the living room, or walk on her tippy toes, or rock back and forth with the music? Yes, all kids do. Does this mean she is going to be the next prima ballerina or Broadway star? No. But I'm a firm believer that every child should dance—boys too! Dance teaches developmental and social skills that will last a lifetime: how to take turns, listen to others, form a circle, and get in a straight line. Dance introduces musicality and physical exercise. You can start dance classes much earlier than sports or school, and

this is often the very first bond of a teacher-student rela-
tionship. We have the advantage of getting kids first—
before they start soccer practice, student council, or
Girl Scouts.

I say enroll your toddler in a dance class and give
it at least two months. If he/she is still kicking and
screaming and disrupting the class, then you know
your child is *not* ready for formal instruction. If he/she
can't wait to get there each week, then you made the
right decision.

. . . .

Dear Abby:
My daughter says her dance teacher picks on her. She always
criticizes her and points out her mistakes. I think I should talk
to the teacher about it and get her off my kid's back. What do
you think?

I think you should send that teacher a thank-you note.
Obviously, your child has some potential. And the teacher is
on her back for a reason. When a child comes home and says
the teacher doesn't even know her name and never corrects
her, consider that a wake-up call. Hint, hint—the teacher
doesn't care because the kid doesn't have it.

Abby
. . . .

PICKING THE RIGHT DANCE TEACHER

No two dance teachers are alike. Some are warm and fuzzy; some are strict and militant; others are clueless and crazy (sound like anyone you know?). For every excellent instructor out there, there is a charlatan, taking your money without providing your child any decent training. Be smart. You are paying for an education, so make sure you get one! Investigate your dance teacher and choose one just the way you would choose your pediatrician. You're going to be trusting these people with your kid's life.

In the United States, dance teachers do not need a license. This is true for all sorts of professionals you might need, from SAT tutors to violin instructors to basketball coaches. You're going to have to vet them yourself. Google the studio online and check out the reviews. Are customers happy and satisfied? Or do they describe the place as filthy, sloppy, and a waste of time and money? Ask friends who have enrolled their kids there. Some studios will let you take a sample class, arrange a tour, and meet with a teacher to get a feel for what's expected. The more you know, the better off you'll be.

Dance is a hands-on art form. This person may be touching your child from the age of three to eighteen. Remember, at the beginning children don't need to excel or be the best in the class—they just need to *love* it! At our studio, children's love for the art of dance (or for whatever they are doing) is what matters! And of course, are you coming back next year?

WHAT MAKES A GOOD/BAD DANCE TEACHER?

The Good Teacher . . .

• Continues his/her own education. Dance is an evolving art. Every month there is a new jump, a new stunt, a new turn. Just like a hairdresser, you need to stay on top of your craft.

• Has the right connections. What pull does the dance teacher have to get your kid that coveted audition?

• Has a well-kept studio. Is it spacious? Is the ceiling high? Does it have Equity-approved floors? Is there a water fountain in the bathroom? All of those things go into choosing the right studio.

• Is focused. Is he/she present for the day-to-day operations? Devoted to the students and able to show your kid the attention he deserves?

• Sees problems and how to fix them. He/she should be able to look at your child and instantly see what is wrong. You don't need another person to pat your kid on the back and tell her how cute she is. You need someone who is going to give it to her straight.

The Bad Teacher . . .

• Is not affiliated with any certified organization such
  as Dance Educators of America or Dance Masters
  of America and is not certified by the United Sports
  Governing Foundation for safety of any acrobatics or
  gymnastics taught in the studio.

• Has a poor track record. No professionals have come
  out of the studio.

• Plays favorites. Only pays attention to one or two
  students (either because they're talented or because
  their moms spend big bucks on lessons) and ignores
  everyone else.

• Has a crappy facility. The studio looks shabby and
  dirty. When was the last time someone washed down
  those gym mats?

• Lacks enthusiasm. This is a dance studio—not a
  sweatshop. Does it feel like fun when you walk in the
  door? Are kids smiling and happy to be there?

GOTTA DANCE!

There are dozens of different dance classes out there for kids, all of which benefit body and mind. Dance helps build and maintain balance, coordination, self-discipline, and physical strength. Plus, it's a great way to express emotions (when kids are having a hard time using their words). Why not let your kid try . . .

Ballet. Ballet requires years of training to learn and master, and much practice to retain proficiency. It has been taught in ballet schools around the world for hundreds of years, and these have historically used their own cultures to transform the art. Ballet is the basis of many types of dance; therefore a good strong foundation is most important. Stylistic variations have emerged and evolved since the Italian Renaissance. Early variations are primarily associated with geographic origin. Examples of this are Russian ballet (including Vaganova), French ballet, and Italian ballet (including Cecchetti). Later variations include contemporary ballet and neoclassical ballet. Perhaps the most widely known and performed ballet style is late-romantic ballet, which is a classical style that focuses on female dancers; features pointe work, and flowing and precise movements; and often presents the female dancers in traditional, short white French tutus.

En pointe means "on the tip" and is a part of classical ballet technique. Pointe is the advancement of ballet class to performing in hard, boxed pointe shoes. The technique developed from the desire for dancers to appear weightless and sylphlike and has evolved to enable dancers to dance on the tips of their toes for extended periods of time. Girls are usually between the ages of nine and twelve years old when they progress to pointe shoes. Most students are ready for pointe when they can hold their turnout from the hips while performing center combinations, hold a proper ballet position (straight back, good turnout, etc.), pull up correctly in the legs, and balance securely in relevé (when a dancer moves from a flat foot to her toes), because dancing en pointe requires one to use the entire body, including the legs, back, and abdominal muscles.

Contemporary. Contemporary dance explores the creative, artistic soul through a strong foundation in ballet and jazz technique. Emphasis is on moving in and out of traditional parallel jazz techniques while picking up on new, subtle movement challenges. This style of dance is constantly changing and evolving with trends in contemporary movement.

Jazz. This is America's true folk dance. The term *jazz* was first applied to a style of music and dance during World War I. Jazz as a dance form, however, originates from the vernacular dances of Africans. This dance form developed alongside jazz music in New Orleans in the early 1900s. In the 1950s, a new genre of jazz dance—modern jazz dance—emerged, with roots in Caribbean traditional dance. Jazz continues to evolve with the changing musical styles of our time. The dance style is heavily influenced by today's fad dances. Other elements of jazz dance are less common and are the stylizations of their respective choreographers. One such example is the inverted limbs and hunched-over posture of Bob Fosse.

Lyrical. This is a style of dance created from the fusion of ballet and jazz dance techniques. It is expressive, simultaneously subtle and dynamic, focused on conveying musicality and storytelling. Choreography is commonly set to popular music, with dramatic vocals as well as rich instrumentation expressing deep personal emotions.

Acrobatics. Acrobatics is the art of doing slow, controlled stunts using the flexibility of the back, legs, and shoulders. The fundamentals include backbends, handstands, elbow stands, chin stands, limbers, and walkovers on both the right and left. As students advance, they add variations of these basics, and when ready, they will begin aerial work to execute each trick without hands.

Gymnastics. Gymnastics is a sport requiring physical strength, agility, coordination, and balance. Movements are executed with a straight back using power and speed. Competitive artistic gymnastics is the best known of the gymnastic sports. It typically involves the women's events of uneven bars, balance beam, floor exercise, and vault. We only work on floor tumbling—from beginner rolls, cartwheels, round-offs, all the way through the more advanced front and back handsprings, tucks, layouts, and twists. Gymnastics evolved from exercises used by the ancient Greeks that included skills for mounting and dismounting a horse, and from circus performance skills.

Contortion. This is a form of extreme acrobatics for dancers born with natural flexibility. We refer to them as "closebenders." If your child is a candidate, he/she will learn additional variations of splits, chin stands, and elbow stands, and a whole vocabulary of amazing tricks.

Hip-hop. A dance fad that is here to stay, this high-energy, athletic, popular dance style originated on the streets in the late eighties with break dancing. There are no rules! Hip-hop has come full circle, incorporating capoeira, martial arts, jazz, and modern dance. In the professional world, dancers must have hip-hop in their repertoire.

Tap. Tap is the only form of dance that incorporates sound. Elementary steps and basic rhythms are taught first, then more intricate patterns and fancier footwork. From Gene Kelly of yesterday to Savion Glover of today, tap remains a driving force in the entertainment field.

Character. Character dance focuses on stylized dance genres that are instantly associated with different recognizable characters such as sailors, cowboys, flappers, and animals. Steps performed include the can-can, hoedown, Charleston, and cakewalk. Character education is vital to any dancer planning to pursue a career in the performing arts.

Musical theater. This is vital training for those students who want to go on to perform on Broadway. A dancer also needs to sing and act. A successful, employable professional is called a "triple threat"! Theater skills, vocal projection, staging, and learning the lyrics to Broadway musicals are all key skills in musical theater.

Partnering. This skill is important when performing in professional productions, where a male dancer will be expected to lead, lift, turn, throw, and catch a female counterpart. The ability to partner safely and confidently is key. Equally, the female dancer must support herself and share in the timing, energy, and cohesive flow from one exciting lift to another.

INSIDE YOUR DANCE BAG

Your dance bag should contain everything you'll need to survive when you're at a dance class or competition. Make sure your dance bag includes . . .

Ballet slippers

Pointe shoes

Black leotard and pink tights

Warm-up sweats or knitties

Colored leotard or dancewear

Band-Aids

Blister bandages

New-Skin liquid bandage

Lots of toe tape

Needle and thread

Scissors

Nail clippers

Thera-Band

Water bottle

Snacks (usually chewy bars or apples)

Icy Hot or Bengay

Clear nail polish (for runs in tights)

iPod/phone/headphones

Character skirt, character shoes, black tights, jazz shoes

All other dance shoes

ABBY'S ULTIMATE ADVICE
Three Key Points to Remember

1. Help your kid find his/her passion. Try new things until something strikes a chord. What is your child good at and excited by, and how can she get even better?

2. Nurture that passion. As a parent, it's your obligation to help your child grow into the best person he can be. Don't assume you know everything, because you don't! Enlist the help of professionals.

3. Not every pro is on the up-and-up. Do some digging. Ask around. Observe teachers in action. Check credentials. If you don't like what you see, find someone else. Your child deserves nothing less than the best.

FIRST POSITION
CROISÉ DEVANT

All's Fair in Dance and War

If you really want to fly, harness your
power to your passion.

—*Oprah Winfrey*

SOME CHILDREN ARE JUST SPECIAL. On my show, that's
Maddie Ziegler. And I am sick and tired of everyone
whining about Maddie. "Maddie has the prettiest outfits!"
"Maddie gets the most attention!" "Maddie's always at the
top of the pyramid!" Well, guess what? Maddie's an exemplary student. She is punctual, prepared, and passionate
about the art of dance. And her example is great for her
peers. Instead of condemning the top kid—the winner,
the champion—your child should be learning from her!
Do what she does well, just the way she does it.

I knew that Maddie was something special the first
time she walked into my studio. She was adorable; that face
was cupcakelike. Her mom introduced herself as Melissa,
and her dad didn't need an introduction. I recognized him
immediately from my old high school days. He gradu-

ated from Penn Hills High School in 1982, and I graduated many, many, many years later (wink). The two looked like a perfect couple with a very sweet, well-behaved, and curious—but still somewhat shy—little girl who was destined to dance. Maddie was only four, but already knew she wanted to take tap and hip-hop. She told me right off the bat she did not want to take ballet or acrobatics. Now, who lets their four-year-old decide how to spend their money? Luckily, at the Abby Lee Dance Company all preschool students are required to take a combination lesson that includes ballet for posture and body alignment, tap for rhythm and timing, and tumbling to build upper body strength and increase flexibility.

Maddie immediately started classes once a week, but Melissa was gung ho and added another day at our satellite studio. Maddie took to all genres of dance, and my staff was abuzz about this smart and talented munchkin. We don't have hip-hop classes for our four- and five-year-old students because there is not that much interest. But Maddie was bright enough to take the mini-hip-hop class with the six- to eight-year-olds, and she was still the smartest kid in the class—picking up the choreography faster than anyone else.

Then Melissa asked if Maddie could just stay another half hour to take the jazz class too! I worried about her ability to get onstage and remember the routines during our annual dance concert, but Maddie made me eat my words. Not only did she retain the choreography, she shone onstage—and continues to shine week after week on national television. So should you be jealous of her? Go right ahead.

We all know life isn't fair. When I say, "All's fair in dance and war," I mean that you pull out all the stops—all the time. You do whatever it takes to win. You dig down deep inside and push yourself to the limit. It also means to be cautious and careful, and know that the people out there whom you're competing against—whether it's in a competition-type setting or in a Broadway show audition—they're going to be nasty, mean, and cruel and you need to be ready for that. The world is not the happiest place. Even getting a job for Disney can be cutthroat.

You can't do this without being prepared. To be prepared, education comes first and foremost. I don't mean learning by the book, I mean getting smart about everything that's going to affect you. This means knowing all about your craft of dancing, and about the choreographer who's hiring the dancers via the casting agency that's writing his/her paycheck. Be knowledgeable going into that situation. If it's a competition, then know everything you possibly can about the people who are judging. What are their backgrounds? Read their bios and find out as much as you can about what they like in a dancer and what they don't like. You should also know everything you can about the facility where you'll be dancing. Is there a stage? What's the flooring on the stage? Is it wood, or marley, or something else?

Dance is not like school. In the dance studio, I always tell my students to copy their (successful) neighbors. Go ahead and steal from them—you're not going to get detention for doing it. In fact, you may just go to the head of the class. This applies to any activity outside of an academic test. If your child is playing chess competitively, and her teammate has a killer seven-step checkmate move, she should memorize it too. That teammate with the sharper moves will help her dig deeper and motivate herself. If your youngster is the strongest one in her class, studio, or gym, it's time to raise the barre. If you don't, you'll both be in for a rude awakening when she heads out to a bigger competition, whether in life, school, or work.

Anything you can learn about what you're doing and what you want to achieve is going to help you in the long run. Who else is going out for the job? What are their talents? What do they have that you don't? All's fair in love and war, and all's fair in dance and war. The more you can find out before you walk into the competition—or up onto the stage—the better.

Now don't get me wrong. Even though I state that all's fair, I do believe that teachers and coaches have to abide by rules of conduct and behavior on behalf of their students, since a child's ability to understand ethical behavior is limited. I'm not talking about extreme situations like what happened between Tonya Harding and Nancy Kerrigan at the 1994 U.S. Figure Skating Championships. I'm talking about how I've seen kids head over to the corner of the studio or stage, throw baby powder on the floor, and stick their feet in it so they can turn faster. When I see something like this happen, I've got to give kudos to the kid for being smart enough to have thought of the old baby powder trick and actually followed through with it. But ethically, it's up to me to stop my students from doing things like this.

When I see something like this happening in a competition, I go right to the people running it and tell them what I saw. And you know that when I do, I'm no shrinking violet—I'm not shy about it one little bit. Not only that, but I *always* tell my kids that if they see foul play and they don't tell me so we can go to the officials, then they shouldn't complain when that kid beats them and they're standing onstage in second place. They had a voice and the power to do something, but they chose not to. I have found that other people aren't so quick to tattle, because "someone won't like them."

When it comes to mean and potentially hateful people, I always tell my kids to be the very best they can be—be better than they are. By being tough on my kids now, I am preparing them for the worst, in dance and in life. As a teacher, I can yell at my students and tell them this, that, and the other thing, I can be mean and nasty, but I never want to hear some other dance teacher talking about my kids negatively. I want to make sure that my students can handle *anything*. If someone is going to tell one of my kids she's fat, or bowlegged, or has horrible posture, tell a girl she's not pretty, or tell a boy he's dancing like a girl, I want to make them so tough and strong that nothing will ever ruffle their feathers—*nothing*!

Kids who have gone on to dance with the Radio City Rockettes, and kids who have gone on to college dance teams, have told me that they have seen a coach or choreographer yelling at the girl next to them and the girl starts to cry, and they're looking at her like "Are you crazy? This is nothing! I was trained by Abby Lee Miller!" Nobody is going to embarrass them and upset them more than I am. I'll do it first, and I'll do it right! But I correct and humiliate them in a private lesson inside my studio. I know just how to push a kid's buttons to get the results I want. I would never do it to them at an audition in front of eight hundred of their peers. All the preparation is done ahead of time to make them tough in any situation.

When I was twenty-two years old, I legally took over my mother's dance studio. Instead of thinking about turning this successful small business into a multimillion-dollar corporation, I was intensely focused on taking the art of dance to a whole new level. My goal was to produce amazing and *employable* dancers—not just amazing dancers. Trust me, there's a huge difference between being a competition kid and someone who can earn a very nice living doing what he or she loves to do. That's what I want for my kids. I want professionalism at all times, so why not train them to be little pros from the start? By the way they behave in class, at competitions, and during performances, they are representing me.

I pride myself on the way I produce a show. Some may call it a recital, but that conjures up dreadful thoughts of tutus on a sweltering summer day in a blazing-hot high school auditorium. We present a dance concert similar to what you would see on Broadway. There's a beginning, a middle, and an end, and it flows seamlessly from one scene to the next—the curtain never closes. At the same time, my kids are learning crucial performance skills: for example, never, ever hit a curtain, because the curtain has dust in it. "So what?" you might ask. The "so what" is that when someone bumps into a curtain onstage, it wiggles and all the dust falls on the sidelights, and guess what happens next? The lights start to smoke, which can make it look like there's a fire. Before you know it, the audience is looking for the exits instead of looking at the dancers on the stage.

My students also learn that backstage is a sacred place. *Never* talk, roughhouse, or even practice. You might distract the performer onstage. Get out of the wings. If you can see the audience, the audience can see you. There are many theatrical rules and even more theater superstitions: for example, don't ever put your shoes on a bed or table, and *never* utter the words *Good luck*. All this protocol is preparing them for their profession. When dancers graduate from my studio, they are 100 percent ready for the entertainment industry. Other dance teachers don't train their students to go on to a professional career in dance—it's like a free-for-all backstage. If you are one of the leggy lovelies selected for the Radio City Christmas

Spectacular, you'd better be on your mark. Six inches in one direction or another could cause you to plummet thirty feet to your death. Everything I teach is for a reason. Someday, when they're working professionally, all these ridiculous rules will come into play. Abby's kids already know what it takes to be a professional.

Break a leg!

. . . .

Dear Abby:
My daughter wanted the lead in her ballet company's production of Nutcracker *but instead is playing one in a large group of mice. She's just devastated, and I don't know what to tell her.*

Here's what you say: "No one ever said life is fair." Do not allow your kid to think she's entitled to be the star of the show, the captain of the team, or the teacher's pet. Make her understand that equality isn't a given. Break it to your kids now: people will get things that you don't. Your boss may one day pass you over for a promotion or fire your butt for no good reason. It's okay to be disappointed. It makes you work harder and fight for what's important to you. That said, as a judge, I look to the backline first—the kids farthest from the front of the stage. I do this because these dancers may not be as strong or as confident as the other dancers. In some competitions, you judge from the balcony so that you can see lines and formations changing. I think your kid should be thrilled that she's in a group. The person in the back on the end should be as strong and talented and polished as the kid front and center. In other words, be the best damn mouse you can be!

Abby

. . . .

BEHIND THE SCENES
My Favorite Dance Moms *Moment*

When I was a young girl growing up in Pittsburgh, my dream was to get a puppy. Every birthday and every Christmas I asked for a puppy—it's all I ever really wanted. But guess what? I never got one. I can remember imagining what it would be like the day my mom or dad would walk into the house with a box, and I would open the box and find a puppy in it. So that's what made it particularly special for me when I gave Mackenzie a puppy on our 2013 Christmas Special show. While I never got the puppy I hoped for when I was growing up, I am grateful that I was able to make Mackenzie's dream come true.

COME PREPARED TO DANCE
The Rules of the Abby Lee Dance Company

Grooming

• We always want to present a polished appearance.

• Hair must be up off the back of your neck and slicked away from the face in either a ponytail, a bun, or a French braid.

• A bun is mandatory for all Tuesday, Thursday, and Saturday ballet classes.

• No jewelry is allowed, for safety reasons. Necklaces can break. Rings can fly off. Earring backs fall.

• No baggy sweats. Neat dance warm-ups may be worn only until your muscles are warm. Young students may wear a sweater if necessary during the winter. Cover-ups must be worn to and from class. Never enter or leave the studio in only your dance attire.

• *Do not* wear dance shoes outside. Wearing dance shoes outside ruins the sole and also tracks dirt, oil, and gravel into the studio, causing damage to the customized dance floors.

Girls Dress Code

• Solid leotard—Any style or material is acceptable, but refrain from purchasing busy patterns.

• Tights—Ballet pink, black, white, light toast, or suntan are permitted. All Tu-Two Cute, Baby Ballerinas, and Prima Preschoolers I may use full footed. Intermediate Prima Preschoolers II need stirrup, footless, or convertible tights. Pink tights are mandatory for all Monday, Tuesday, Thursday, and Saturday ballet classes.

• No Tights—Bare legs are mandatory for Monday Legs and Feet/Jazz Class.

• Hair—Long hair must be up and secured off the back of the neck for technique as well as prevention of injury to another dancer.

Boys Dress Code

• Pants—Black dance pants, sweatpants, or hip-hop pants.

• Tops—Tucked in T-shirt or muscle shirt.

> **NOTE:** All male students should be respectful of all the ladies in this building, as well as their property and the building itself. You are here on a partial tuition scholarship. Many of the girls are

paying five times this. Your behavior should be exemplary at all times, and scholarship recipients should always work harder in class than anyone else. You will be held to a higher standard by all faculty members. The first time you are asked to leave a class because of your behavior, your tuition will be changed to the full price from the current Reign Dance Productions tuition rate chart.

Class Behavior

We want all our students to have an enjoyable and educational dance experience. We will treat you and your children with courtesy and respect. We expect our students to show the same attitude toward their teachers and fellow dancers. We request that your children observe the following simple rules:

• Pay attention to your teacher. Don't talk with your friends during class! It disrupts the whole class and makes it difficult for the teacher to communicate with the students. Meet your friends before or after class for social fun.

• Food and drinks are permitted in the *den* (our dressing room/storage area) *only*. Be careful—spills ruin the floors and food attracts bugs. You may have snacks in the den, but please dispose of your trash properly. There are breaks for water during shoe changes. Don't even think about bringing a water bottle into the studio.

• Do not pull up on or hang from the ballet barres.
  They can be pulled from the wall or you can get
  stuck in them. Barres are for balance and support.
  Come prepared to dance—attire, grooming, attitude,
  ambition, energy!

Classroom Etiquette

Reasonable rules and standards are provided to
promote self-discipline. Students should arrive at the
school with sufficient time to change into dance shoes
to begin class on time. Students who arrive ten minutes
after the scheduled class time are welcome to observe
the class; however, they will not be permitted to
participate unless there is an extenuating circumstance.
If students need to leave before the end of the class, they
should notify the teacher before class begins. Students
may not leave the classroom without first receiving
permission from the teacher.

Teachers have the responsibility to see that their class
is under control, and they have the authority to dismiss
any student who will not cooperate and is a disruption to
the rest of the class. Inappropriate dress or behavior will
not be allowed. No gum, food, or drinks will be permitted
inside the classrooms during class or rehearsal.

Your children are a reflection of you.
Good manners and proper etiquette are always expected.

SOME PEOPLE ARE BORN LUCKY

My friend Sandy tells me all the time that I was born under a lucky star. I don't know that I agree with her—I think I've had plenty of bad luck in my life, like locking my keys in the car while it's running, or losing my cell phone when it's dead, or getting two parking tickets in one afternoon. She may be talking about the times when she drags me kicking and screaming to bingo and then I win the grand prize. Or when the headpieces aren't there in the box of costumes and I whip up something that's ten times better than what we had to begin with. Or getting my own reality television show. Is there a star following me, or is it star quality? Do I really believe in luck? Maybe just dumb luck. Maybe it was all my years of preparation meeting this wonderful opportunity. I'm sure millions envy my success. Others may be blessed with good looks, or a great body, or a photographic memory—I was blessed with common sense.

Some may call it luck—I call it destiny. I believe we are all following a script. Somebody's master plan. My life itself is a dance that has been choreographed. I am just doing what I'm supposed to do. Now if everyone in my world did what they were supposed to do, there would be peace, or at least a few less headaches.

It's just a fact—some dancers are better than others. Is it because they're lucky? I don't know. Maybe, maybe not. They may have a particular facility—the perfect body, beautiful feet, or pretty legs. Maybe your kid is a little swaybacked, round-shouldered, knock-kneed, pigeon-toed, or bowlegged. Maybe she's not super agile or athletic. That's a problem, because the less natural, God-given talent a dance student has, the harder it will be for her to excel. Maybe she will have to develop a work ethic far superior than that of the girl who's always at the top. And when I say hard work, I don't mean just time. I mean blood, sweat, and tears. *Literally.*

And it can all change. Through the years I have come to realize that some of the youngsters who start out so strong—who have the built-in tools to excel, and to win every competition possible—don't always end up going on to a professional career as a dancer. But the child who doesn't always win, the kid who comes in second or even third—the dancer who has to work really hard for every achievement—is more often than not the one who continues to persevere through the challenges and ends up in the spotlight as an adult.

I can't tell you who's going to end up being an amazing dancer, because there are other factors that come into play, but I can tell you who *should* be an amazing dancer. It's that kid with the natural turnout and flexibility in her back, strong shoulders and hyperextended legs with perfectly arched feet and the same measurement from the hip to the knee as the knee to the ankle. Is her rib cage distended or closed? Let's not forget the looks. Adorable, stunning, exotic, interesting. All those things go into making a beautiful dancer, and I consider those kids born lucky.

In Russia and Romania, they look for certain characteristics and body types in young children. When they find those kids with the perfect bodies for dance or gymnastics, they groom them to become the best, and the families of those kids receive benefits. I'm sure those parents consider themselves very lucky to have a child who was born with the right body type and was selected to become an elite athlete, because it's their ticket to the good life. They're supplied with a roof over their heads, an education, food, and the best training money can buy. I personally think that instead of trying out all sorts of activities to see what your child likes, it makes more sense just to find out what they're good at. Let's face it—kids like to be great. It would save parents a lot of time and energy if we borrowed some of the Romanians' methods. Kids like things that come easily to them, that's a given. When it stops being fun, do you bail? When a straddle split starts to hurt, when the girl next to you effortlessly lifts her leg up to her ear, or when your best friend starts beating you on a consistent basis, do you throw in the towel? Not so fast . . . this activity is not just part of your life; it describes you as a person. So you hang in there for a while.

Some lucky kids have the natural ability that God gave them through their parents' genes. But while these kids might all have the promise of becoming amazing dancers, they may not have a mom and dad who care about their dancing, fencing, or skating. They may not have the finances to pursue anything more than a one-hour class each week. They may not have the enthusiasm or the musicality to perform passionately. They may not care about excelling at anything.

Then, on the flip side, that same kid with the great body for dancing might be really good at something else too. He might be a great athlete, or really smart to the point where he's attending college at the same time he's attending high school. So you know who should pursue dancing, but you don't know if they're in for the long haul. You can only guide them, and take an interest in them, and tell their parents that they "have what it takes" to become a great dancer, artist, athlete, or rocket scientist.

Did your child arrive with the genetic makeup to become something fabulous, special, above and beyond the average? Then yes, absolutely, your child has huge potential to be a success story, and you would be crazy not to push your kid down that path!

Believe it or not, when the TV show *Dance Moms* was originally cast, they didn't choose my cream of the crop. They didn't even look at my national title winners. The kids on the TV show did not audition. Their mothers were interviewed, and the show was supposed to be more about the moms than the dancers. The dancing was supposed to be about one-eighth of the show, and I was originally on camera only as a choreographer. With the exception of the short-lived Vivi-Anne, the kids chosen for the show were all students of mine from the age of two and a half, except one little girl who arrived in Season Two, and she had already been at my studio. She's actually the only regular who had to audition. The other kids never danced a step; they submitted video of their best thirty seconds. Thirty moms were chosen from my studio to be interviewed for the show. Out of those initial moments on camera, they picked only five moms and one wicked witch.

If you look at my computer, there's a file folder on the desktop labeled "Pictures for John TV." This was the original folder that I sent to that hot guy in L.A., John Corella, when he first mentioned his idea for a TV show. It's a little scary to open that folder, for it contains the headshots of the girls who ended up on the show. He actually created the premise for the TV show *Abby's Ultimate Dance Competition* first. That's the show John and I wanted to do originally, but who was going to listen to us?

And then there was the casting director who took all the credit for casting the five moms and their daughters when in fact we had already chosen the five moms. They sent in their own photos and videos from competitions and uploaded Flip-cam footage every night. There they were, ready to be filmed for the show when the casting director arrived. When this casting director made that claim, I said, "What do you mean, you cast the show? You came to Pittsburgh, you walked into my studio, and there were five moms and you put them on TV. You didn't cast them. You didn't go out and find them. They were sitting there waiting for you. You had appointments, and you were late."

The kids chosen for the TV show are all adorable and built nicely, but not one of them has the signature Abby Lee feet. When you look back at the history of the ALDC, I always had the pretty girls, the best-dressed girls, the well-behaved girls. However, my groupings always fit together somehow and made sense. For a few years it was the tall blondes who could turn and tumble. The next generation was four dark-haired debs with incredible flexibility. A few years later came an all-American, wholesome team of Trinas. But one thing remained the same: the look, the height, the impeccable technique, and the two-year age range.

What were these producers thinking? Did any of them know anything about dance? What was I going to do with this team of misfit toys? Were they casting a new version of the *Facts of Life* TV show, or a competitive dance team? Some taller than others, some skinnier than others, some older than others, and some way better than others?

. . . .

Dear Abby:
I think our dance coach is pushing our daughter way too
hard. She's only nine and the coach wants her to be on pointe
this year. Not to mention in class with girls twelve and
thirteen years old. I feel bad holding her back, but this seems
like too much.

There are lots of philosophies on beginning pointe work. The role of Clara in the Radio City Christmas Spectacular is for a child who is four feet eight or under. Not too many twelve- and thirteen-year-olds are under four feet eight. Girls that height are usually nine or ten. If your child is going to begin on pointe younger, like nine or ten, perhaps only fifteen minutes a week, after a ballet class, would be okay. Check with her pediatrician. In my opinion, nothing more than half an hour, twice a week.

Abby

. . . .

YOU HAVE TO WORK YOUR BUTT OFF TO BE THE TOP OF THE PYRAMID

There's working hard, and then there's working smart. First of all, you have to work smart. If you do it right the first time, you won't have to do it over and over. Dance is a physical art, not a sport. It takes years of technical training, sore muscles, bleeding feet, blisters, bruised knees, scabs, sweat, and tears—it takes all of that, and more. So if you don't have the will to work to achieve greatness, to look in the mirror at yourself and know that you have to leap higher, then stay home. If you stand at the ballet barre and have your leg up in the air and see that the girl in front of you has her leg higher and you don't want to work toward that or to be better than she is, then stay home.

I remind my girls that if you're not giving it your all, then you're taking up space that someone else could be using. Maddie attended a regular public school for the first five or six years of her schooling and did well. Now she has chosen to be homeschooled and has private ballet class every morning at 9:30 A.M. She has six other private lessons, and she takes the senior company–level classes when we're not shooting. As a result, she has improved dramatically. Maddie is smart, and now she's better than all the other girls on the TV show. This isn't because she's my favorite, it's because she has worked hard and made it to the top of the pyramid and can physically out-dance all the other girls. It's that simple.

To be honest, the other kids on the show aren't as driven. They tell Maddie to go for it and act as if they don't even care. They say, "We aren't going to try to compete with you, Maddie. You can just carry the show for another twenty-six episodes." You have to really work your butt off to succeed. There's always someone else, somewhere else, working harder and putting in more time.

ABBY'S MYSTERY MAN
by John Corella

Abby and I had this crazy idea of showcasing the world of dance competitions with girls and their moms. We took the idea to Bryan Stinson, a television producer who then became the cocreator of *Dance*

Moms. I was a competitive dancer (Mr. Dance of America, 1994). I used to beat Abby's kids all the time—that's how I met her. She was younger than all the other dance teachers. She was fun, cool, and a little bit flirty. Abby's main objective has always been to make her dancers stars, so when I told her this reality show had the green light from a production company, of course she was the first person to submit her dancers to me. She was on it.

At the time, the idea for the show was to move from city to city in each episode, looking at different kids and moms in each location, and a dance teacher wasn't really involved. But as we developed the show, we decided to focus on Abby's studio, and on Maddie, Paige, Chloe, Mackenzie—and of course their moms. It turns out there was enough crazy to keep us in Pittsburgh.

To me, Abby is the ultimate dance mom. She doesn't have kids, but she can do something that the moms can't do, and the moms have something she doesn't have, so they work well together. Abby is the superglue of the show. She's smart, she's outrageous, she's courageous, she's funny, and she's got a heart of gold. Make no mistake about it: she's a tough teacher, but believe me—she's not the only dance instructor I've seen who teaches the way she does. She is, however, the only one I know who's courageous enough to own up to it. She'll be the first to admit that her approach might not be politically correct, but it works for her. Throughout my professional career, I have shared both stage and screen with several of Abby's alumni. Her kids get in front of an audience and they're incredible. And that's all the proof I needed.

John Corella is the creator and executive producer of *Dance Moms*—without him, there would be no *Dance Moms* television show. John used to be a competitive dancer, and he and Abby used to run into each other at different competitions across the country. She likes to keep her enemies close, so they eventually became colleagues.

> *You know you're a dance mom when . . .*
> *you have rhinestones and E-6000*
> *(an industrial-strength adhesive) in your purse.*
>
> You know you're a dancer when . . .
> you can keep your hair in a bun for four days straight!
>
> You know you're a diva when . . . you carry a Louis Vuitton
> bag at age nine, and everybody knows your name.

Dancers used to say their mothers were living vicariously through them, and I believe that's true to an extent,
but more and more, I see a parent's work ethic in the kid.
If you have a mom who sits on her ass in the dance studio
for five hours a day and talks about people behind their
backs, she's lazy and her kid turns out to be lazy too. The
kid is yawning and constantly looking at the clock. She's
in the room with her leotard on—she actually showed
up—but she doesn't want to do the work.

Then you have another parent who works two or
three jobs in addition to volunteering at the studio. This
is the parent who bends over to pick up the trash off the
floor of the studio and puts it in the trash can—instead
of ignoring it. The children of these parents are the ones
who work hard.

I have taught poor kids and wealthy kids, and what I
see is that when a parent is a hard worker—whether poor
or wealthy—her kids tend to be hard workers too. You
can have kids who are poor, whose parents treat them
like they're kings, giving them everything they want, and
they're lazy. I may push and challenge a child mentally
and physically, but ultimately those kids have to go out
onstage and do that dance, because nobody can do it for
them, and I can't make them do it. You can't stick a gun
to their heads and make them work harder to become
better—they have to want it. Even when parents sign
their kids up for extra classes hoping that will make them
better dancers, if those kids don't want it bad enough, all

the classes in the world aren't going to help them become stars. So even though a mom is living through her kid, the mom can't make the kid do something the kid doesn't want to do.

I've never seen any of the lazy girls become motivated, but I have seen kids who weren't great dancers, and who weren't born with the ideal dancer's physique or facility, who worked so hard that they became great dancers. I had a young man who was (and I say this with great love) a dorky little kid with a big grin and big ears, and he was a twin. His twin sister danced, as did his older sister, and he was just thrown into it. I thought his mother was a bitch on wheels. She looked at him and basically said, "You can either dance or you can stay home because I'm not driving anywhere else."

Anyway, this kid was very close to me—I feel like I raised him. One time in the late eighties we were all going on a cruise for a dance competition and convention that took us away for most of a summer and he couldn't go. His mother couldn't take the kids on the cruise so he was out of luck. When we came back, he had both splits down on the floor and was dancing so much better that I thought he'd been going to another studio behind my back. I asked him what he did to improve so much and he said he had worked by himself at home the entire summer. He then went on to say to me that he would never stay home again. He said, "You're never leaving me—I'm going with you from now on, and I'll get a scholarship to every convention so I can go with you." He is now the dance supervisor for the Broadway show *Wicked*, in charge of every single *Wicked* in the world. He teaches every new person coming into any *Wicked* show, and he shows them what they're supposed to do. He's done six hundred Broadway shows by now. He's so valuable to them that they let him do movies and commercials and other Broadway shows because they can't teach anyone else everything that he knows. So this is what I mean by your kid has to want it because nobody can want it for him or her. No amount of overzealous parents paying for extra classes is going to make a better dancer. Only the child can become a better dancer if he or she wants it.

This is of course a lot more than most kids are willing to give. That can be a problem for a child who's always saying, "But my friends don't practice violin three hours a day," or "Susie gets to watch TV instead of going to rehearsal." This can also be a problem for the mom, who comes to me and complains, "Susie has a solo, and my daughter doesn't!" Don't tell me that your kid should do something because her friend is doing it. To be competitive, your child will have to *not* do what her girlfriends are doing. Forget Susie. Because when Susie gets a full ride to Harvard, she's not worrying about your kid!

. . . .

Dear Abby:

My five-year-old loves to dance, but I'm a single mom. I don't have any extra money to spend on dance classes—I'm barely paying my rent and electric bill every month. What should I do?

You want my honest opinion? Take the deadbeat father to court and make him pay for lessons. Every kid needs to dance! That said, you can also contact a studio in your area and ask if there is any financial aid, payment plan, or scholarship package available. Where there's a will, there's a way, and most studios know not everyone is loaded. Reach out.

Abby

. . . .

A LITTLE COMPETITION IS GOOD FOR YOU

I firmly believe that a little competition is good for you. I once heard a coach tell his team, "Off the field, we're friends. On the field, we're warriors." Good for him! I believe a healthy dose of competitiveness is a great motivator.

I believe that competition starts in kindergarten. It begins with whose coloring-book page did the teacher put on the bulletin board. In an effort to take the competition element away, parents take their kids to dance studios that are noncompetitive. They have their kids participate in activities like swim lessons, but they don't join the swim team because it's too competitive. They want to encourage their child to play T-ball because everybody gets a trophy. These parents don't realize it, but their children are already competing academically. They're competing for someone's attention, most likely their teacher. They're competing when that mom dresses her child for school in the morning and makes sure that she has a giant bow in her hair or that she has her best Christmas sweater on for the Christmas party. They are competing with what they are wearing to be the cutest or best dressed. They just don't want to admit it.

A little competition is healthy. Kids who are home-schooled don't know what it feels like to get that paper back in front of the rest of your class with big red marks on it. It's embarrassing. Or, on the flip side, when they do get the A+ and it's in a big circle with a smiley face next to it on their paper. When you're homeschooled, you don't have your best friend looking over your shoulder with envy because you got the best grade in the class, so you don't get the glory or the embarrassment. As for Maddie, who is homeschooled, this works out wonderfully because she is competing in dance every single weekend.

I think both glory and embarrassment help to shape a child's personality. The kid who isn't doing so well needs to buckle down and concentrate more, and the kid who's doing well deserves the praise for having the highest score in the class. In my dance class, every kid who walks into my room to take a class is competing against everyone else in there every minute. I think the mirror can be both your best friend and your toughest competitor. When you look in the mirror and see someone leaping across the floor and she's higher than you by a foot, then you need to compete against that person by jumping higher than she does the next time you go across the floor. I am always screaming at the girls to look into the mirror because I know they will compete against one another if they have to work hard to keep up with and be better than the others. The competition that happens when they are looking in the mirror and comparing themselves with others makes them better dancers.

A lot of dance teachers, especially young ones, ask me, "What should I do? I just opened a dance studio and right now we're noncompetitive, but some of the parents who have seen your show have been asking me if I would consider competitions for my students." I always tell them that competition can make your dancers tremendous and really motivate them to be better *or* it can ruin your business. If the kids at your studio see kids from another studio down the street performing better at competitions, then those kids are going to walk.

And it depends on what you're in it for. I was never in it to make a million dollars. I was in it to produce employable kids. I always wanted to be able to say that I produced the most employable dancers. I made that possible. Most of my dancers didn't leave my studio and go to NYU or

Carnegie Mellon for four years; they went from my studio to Fifty-First Street between Eighth and Ninth Avenues in New York City, got an apartment, went to an audition, and got the job. I know that I did that for them. Had their parents chosen another studio in town, they'd still be here in Pittsburgh doing something else. Maybe flipping burgers at McDonald's or working at the mall.

. . . .

Dear Abby:
I think my six-year-old son is an amazing dancer. Should he be competing or performing?

The only way to know if you've given birth to the next Baryshnikov is to take him to a dance class. You're his mom, so you can't be objective. He sneezes and you applaud. That's why you should leave it to the professionals. I can tell when a child is naturally talented by his physical attributes. Do his hip sockets turn out? Do his legs hyperextend? Do his feet arch the way they are supposed to in classical dance? All these things along with the desire, the dedication, and the determination go into making a champion in the dance world.

Abby

. . . .

BEHIND THE SCENES
A Day in the Life

For *Dance Moms,* I usually head to the studio at about noon. I get into hair and makeup and talk briefly about the ideas and music. I start teaching at about 3:00 P.M., and we go all the way until the last class ends at 10:00 P.M. that night. My business day doesn't start or end at the dance studio. I'm always working on costumes, placing orders, or searching for music at home, either late at night or early in the morning. The day-to-day activity of running a business takes up most of my morning. Then I eat lunch and head to the studio. I had to cut back on my teaching because of the demands of the show, but more important, I had to cut back to spend more time with my mother, whose health started to fail before she passed away in February. At the end of the classes, we usually have "Abby After Class," which is a time to dish at my front desk with the other dance teachers, to reflect on the day, and for me to hear what's going on with the other classes, students, and mothers. I'm a night owl. Once I head home at 10:30 or 11:00 P.M., I'm up for three or four more hours doing paperwork and all the other business that wasn't taken care of before I went to the studio.

I'm lucky to have an amazing group of instructors. Every one of my instructors is on the same page. They follow a curriculum that was created by my mother more than fifty years ago for all the preschool classes. We have a great team at my studio, Reign Dance Productions, and the Abby Lee Dance Company. In addition to dance, we offer voice lessons and acting classes.

When we're on the road for a competition, we've got an entirely different routine. Here's a typical schedule for the Abby Lee Dance Company during a Saturday competition, though the times can change quite a bit depending on the specific event:

> 5:30 A.M.: Wake up.
> 6:00–8:00 A.M.: Hair and makeup.
> 8:00–9:00 A.M.: Breakfast; then on the bus to the competition.
> 9:00 A.M.: Competition starts.
> 6:00 P.M.: Awards ceremony.

And win or lose, there's always drama with the moms—*guaranteed*.

It would probably surprise most *Dance Moms* fans to find out that we don't get to see the episodes before they are shown on the air. I see them when everyone else does.

SIBLING RIVALRY IS A PLUS

Often you will find two or more siblings in the same dance studio, even on the same competitive team. Sometimes it's just because it's more convenient for Mom—less chauffeuring to do. Stop, drop, and roll. But other times it's because they genuinely care for one another and they want to help their siblings become better dancers.

When you have a sibling, you have built-in competition. There is also the case where the younger sister isn't starting out on the same playing field as the older child, and she has a leg up on her peers. When the younger sister of one of my students is dragged to the dance studio daily, and grows up in that environment—drinking from the water fountain, visiting the ladies' room, and getting candy from the snack machine—she becomes very familiar with the surroundings. So by the time she's two and a half or three years old and it's time to go into the classroom, she isn't hanging on her mother's leg screaming her lungs out, because she already knows that you're supposed to go into that room, listen to the teacher, and have fun.

Usually Little Sis is way ahead of the game. She has absorbed proper terminology just by hearing the words plié and relevé, and if she's on the ball, she has already learned how to do those ballet basics from Big Sis. When children are very close together in age, the older sibling ends up speaking for the new baby, reaching to get her what she wants, and even physically making her do the ever-important first arabesque. Younger siblings know all the positions before they ever get into the classroom. This usually means the younger sibling will turn out better. If not better, certainly smarter. That's definitely what's happened with Mackenzie.

Siblings are great because you have someone to practice with. You have someone to play your music while you're rehearsing, and then you play her music while she runs through her number. For all those exercises that require a partner, you have someone to practice with. If you have a conflict, like a school activity you have to go to, then your sibling can come in and learn your part and teach it to you when you get home that night, so the next day when you go to class you already know it. You always have a built-in duet partner and don't have to rely on anyone else.

I have two families on my show with siblings, Brooke and Paige and Maddie and Mackenzie. I frequently tell Mackenzie, in an effort to motivate her to do better, that when Maddie was her age, she was already doing this or that. Guess what? *It works!*

Jealousy is almost always a big part of sibling relationships. Especially when kids are young, it's hard not to be jealous. Whether they are the oldest, youngest, or middle child, everyone is vying for Mommy's attention. This can be a good thing because it drives them—it makes them push themselves harder and faster to come in first. There is a natural competition that already exists at home, so it's easy to bring it to the dance floor. I've seen this with Maddie and Mackenzie. While the girls are supportive of each other, they also want me and their mom, Melissa, to be proud of them. If one wins and the other doesn't, it's a tough pill to swallow.

I do believe, however, that the second child has an advantage. The first one knows how to say her ABCs. Little Sis might not know all her colors yet, but she can order off the yellow-and-red McDonald's drive-thru menu! Why? Because she's savvy—and she's observant of what's going on around her. I have come to the conclusion that in dance, the younger sibling begins at a younger age and therefore gets into the swing of things much quicker. In the history of the Abby Lee Dance Company, the younger sibling has often surpassed the competition records and the professional experience of his or her older role model.

Except of course in the case of Brooke and Paige. Brooke was the Maddie of her time. She was winning everything, everywhere. She was cute and little and talented! Her mom, Kelly, carried her on her hip like a baby until she was ten years old. Where was Paige? I don't know, maybe in the car? Those kids are only three years apart with a brother in the middle. Shouldn't she have been one of the siblings learning by osmosis? My theory is that Paige was so pretty, maybe her parents didn't think talent would ever really matter. Or maybe Kelly pushed so hard and sacrificed so much for Brooke that when the next kids came along, she was exhausted. Whatever the reason, some of the kids play second fiddle to the firstborn.

ABBY'S ULTIMATE ADVICE
Three Key Points to Remember

1. Life isn't fair. Some people are naturally attractive, smart, and talented. I know that sucks for all the rest of us, but it's a hard, cold fact—pretty counts!

2. Competition is a good thing. It may stress you out, but it also makes you work hard, stay focused, and push yourself further.

3. No one *deserves* to win. It isn't your God-given right. Entitled you are not. You have to eat, sleep, breathe your dream—achieving one goal after another to reign supreme. Nothing your mom says is going to change that.

SECOND POSITION
À LA QUATRIÈME DEVANT
Everyone's Replaceable

> Winning isn't everything—it's the only thing!
> —*Henry Russell Sanders*

I DON'T CARE HOW GOOD your kid is (or how good you *think* she is). For every one of her, there are ten more girls nipping at her heels, waiting to take her place. That means she constantly has to step it up to stay where she is. We teach new things in every class. Dance is a constantly evolving art. I expect my kids to be on their toes!

This goes for life as well. If we've learned anything from the economic mess the United States recently fell into, it's that this is the rule. Companies can be downsized; people are disposable if some person or machine can do it better and easier and cheaper. Teaching your children this lesson early on will help them handle life's little—and not-so-little—ups and downs with grace and dignity.

Do your job. Do it the best you can. Do it right, because somebody, sometimes your best friend, is waiting for you to screw up so she can take your place. I am replaceable. I'm not the best dance teacher in the world. I'm not the only dance teacher in the world. I just feel like there's always somebody who's one step ahead of me. I go to bed at night with my head spinning, full of ideas and stuff to do to help my students become more successful. (But when some mom from Pittsburgh who knows nothing—who's never been to a Broadway show, who's never traveled to L.A. or stayed at the Beverly Hills Hotel or even been inside the Polo Lounge—questions my judgment? That's like challenging my life's vocation, lady! When I was a kid, my mom or dad dropped me off at my clarinet lesson, my drama classes, or the roller rink. What happened to paying the professional to do her job? What happened to entrusting the expert with your child? What happened to respect?)

During one of the episodes on the show, one of the girls—Payton—got hurt in the wings literally three minutes before going onstage. The paramedics had to come, put her on a gurney, and wheel her away. We pulled the kids away from the entire situation, and they reblocked the spacing and then went out and danced. They won their division, and then they won the high score of the entire day at the competition. I told my kids, "See, Payton was replaced by nobody—do you realize how easily Payton was replaced?" Some kid piped up and whined no one replaced her and I said, "That's right, we didn't need anybody to replace her—get it?" The lightbulb went on in their pretty little heads. They understood in that one defining moment that they were all replaceable. I truly believe that if you aren't on your toes every minute of every day, then you will be replaced. And even then, you may be anyway.

· ·

Dear Abby:
We left our dance studio a year ago to go to another one, but now my daughter is bored and wants to come back. I hate begging . . . what should I do?

You don't have to beg. You might just have to pay up front in full. Nobody will want to take another chance on your child after she went to a competing studio. You'd be surprised. But all dance teachers are running a business, and we have to look at your child as a paying customer.

Abby
· ·

BEHIND THE SCENES
Elton John's Oscar Party and Jennifer Lawrence

While I've lost track of the number of battle wounds I have suffered dealing with all the mama drama on *Dance Moms,* I'm grateful for all the good things that have come my way. Today we can be seen in most every American family's living room, and our show airs in thirty-two other countries. Just imagine me screaming in all those different languages! I am thrilled that so many more children are taking dance lessons because of me and the ALDC. Many more people know about dance now because of the show. One year we were in a limo headed to Elton John's party while Jennifer Lawrence was on the red carpet at the pre-Oscar festivities— talking about *Dance Moms*! Our phones were on fire, jumping and buzzing out of our hands, because everyone was watching the live Oscar telecast at home on TV and calling to tell us that she had mentioned *Dance Moms.* One time I was able to take my entire senior company to the Teen Choice Awards. It was a special treat, a gift for them. For a bunch of kids from Pennsylvania, that's a big deal. And I've got to admit that seeing my face on a billboard towering five stories over Hollywood Boulevard was surreal. Pretty damn good for a middle-aged dance teacher from Pittsburgh.

TAKE YOUR WORK SERIOUSLY

I think a lot of parents who have their children enrolled in a dance class look at it as just a hobby or an after-school activity—something they can take or leave. To dance instructors, it's way more than that. It's what they do, it's what they love, it's their job, it's their livelihood, and they take it most seriously. Parents should think of their monthly tuition payment as an investment. It may be a nominal amount for a recreation class once a week, or a hefty chunk of change for a serious dance student. Either way, you are paying for a service, and you should make sure you are getting your money's worth.

I have thirty-three years' experience in the business. If I were a math teacher at a public school, I could retire with a pension and benefits for the rest of my life, but rats, I chose to be a dance teacher because this is what I love to do. I expect my students and their parents to love it too. Children should certainly enjoy the activity and have fun during their time at the dance studio or ball field or gym or basketball court—wherever they are—but they should also show you what they learned, they should practice at home, and they should improve each month.

NOTE: Don't ask if you have to pay for the lesson when your child was absent. Dumb question—of course you do! The teacher was there, the building was open, the lights were on, and all the bills still need to be paid.

A dancer's life is often short lived, while golfers can

compete well into their sixties. At the same time your peers are preparing for college, *you* are preparing for your career. Some kids change their majors two or three times, others switch schools—moving from state to state. And even after graduating, many young men and women work at a couple different jobs before getting their first big job that pays well. My kids get their first big break right out of high school. While your friends are trying to find themselves in college, you are getting a paycheck, week after week. Your four years of high school training with the Abby Lee Dance Company are intense in the dance world. This is why it's really important that the dancers and their parents take this very seriously and why dance instructors take their jobs so seriously. Unlike most job-fair options, your chosen profession is fast and furious. You're going a thousand miles an hour on Day One.

Whether your child dances for me or tumbles for Béla Károlyi or plays for Juilliard, she will be representing an institution, and everything that's gone into building that reputation, every time she performs, competes, or just introduces herself. She will have to ask herself, "What is appropriate behavior?" And you, the parent, will have to help her develop confidence and good manners (more on this later). She's going to be part of something bigger than herself. My students work hard to earn the red Abby Lee Dance Company jacket, and they better act appropriately or they don't get to wear the jacket anymore. There's no smoking, no drinking, no swearing, and certainly no slouching when you are wearing my name across your back! When you are representing me, it's decorum at all times and proper etiquette always applies.

. . . .

Dear Abby:

Because my eleven-year-old daughter has excelled at dancing, her teacher has moved her up to a team with older girls who talk about boys a lot and are texting constantly. I don't want my daughter to be exposed to this stuff at such a young age. What should I do?

This is something you really can't control. If your daughter needs to dance with these kids, she needs to bond with them, and she's certainly going to be in the dressing room or in the studio lounge as well as in rehearsals with them. You can't protect your child from the big, bad world. Make sure her friends at school and in the neighborhood remain the same age as your daughter. Don't "OK" the movies or football games with these dance teens in front of the Friday night lights. I think you need to instill good values in your child at home that she will carry with her the rest of her life. You can't take the kid out of the bad—you have to take the bad out of the kid. Hopefully your kid is a good one who's not going to be led astray.

Abby

. . . .

PULL YOUR OWN WEIGHT

On the junior elite competition team you see on TV, there's one little girl who's outstanding and can carry the group numbers most of the time. Choreographically we create formations so that the judges' eyes go to her. Whether she's in a different color, or whether she does a solo-turn section while everyone else is posing, the judges can't take their eyes off her!

I feel like some of the kids on the TV show aren't pulling their own weight; they're letting someone else do the dance for them. We have to put pressure on them to make them realize that on a team everyone is important, even if you're the kid in the back or the kid on the end, because some judges' eyes might look your way. If judges happen to be in the balcony, they're going to look for the precision in the formations and everyone on the team as a whole. This is why it's so important for everyone on the team to be at the same outstanding technical level.

We all know when someone on the team isn't giving her all. Why the rest of the girls don't say anything, I'll never know. They don't bicker among themselves—they're nice and polite at all times. They really love one another. They're just starting to hit those tween years and that teenager stuff, so the mean girls might begin to surface. Some of the moms are starting to realize that I have a problem with the fact that all the kids get the same stipend whether they win or lose. Last season, Maddie had seventeen solos and Paige only did one—go figure. This goes back to life isn't fair: Maddie works her butt off and gets the same stipend for the show as the other dancers who don't work nearly as hard. Money is a motivator; if the network gave out bonuses for every win, maybe *every* kid would win.

I run my dance teams that are not part of the reality TV show, but a part of *my* reality, very differently. It's my job to teach them a lesson! I call out each student, making her perform a group routine by herself in front of her peers because I know she *can't*. Then when she stops and forgets the next step and everybody in the number is looking at her, it's embarrassing. No teacher enjoys making a mockery of a child, but sometimes I'm left with no other option. Sometimes, instead of taking the hint and practicing, the child just quits. Regardless, her parents still have to pay through the end of the year.

· ·

Dear Abby:

What should the rest of us moms do about another mom who never shows up on time and never helps with "team stuff"?

Either you evenly distribute her weight among the other moms, or you feel sorry for the child and you take on her parent's responsibility, or you can quit putting up with the freeloader and lobby the other mothers to pitch in to cover the child's tuition, as long as the teacher throws her out. You can't expect the teacher to throw her out and lose money.

Abby

· ·

BE HUMBLE

As a dancer, or any kind of "star," you have to be humble and you have to be easy to work with. You have to be approachable. The coach wants you to be a good role model and a leader other dancers can look up to. Being humble is admirable, but you can't be embarrassed about winning either. You can't take the trophy and hold it down by your side so that no one will notice it. The people who own and run the competition want you to jump up and down and be excited about winning. There's a very fine line between being humble, or modest, and embarrassed. We want you to be proud. We want you to be happy that you won—you worked hard—but you can't get cocky, nasty, and rub it in anyone's face.

You got an A on your algebra test. Good for you. There are lots of other kids getting As on their tests too. What makes you any better? What makes you stand out from the rest? If you truly want to excel and be better than everyone around you, you have to push yourself further or have a coach who will do it for you.

Some kids just aren't confident, they have low self-esteem and they question their abilities. I find that the kid with balls, the kid with tenacity, the kid who's going to go into that audition and work her way to the front and who says, "I'm the best one and you have to hire me," often doesn't have the talent to back it up. There, on the other side of the room way in the back, is an awesome dancer with an adorable look and all the right moves, but she doesn't have the confidence, the guts, or the diva attitude. That is hard to teach—believe me, I've tried. You just hope that one day that kid will realize if she doesn't push her way to the front, she'll never be seen. If kids don't risk getting shot down, they'll never know what it's like to stand tall. If they don't put their heart out on the platter, they'll never know if someone's going to love them.

When I have a dancer who is full of herself (I don't have to explain that, do I?), I'm quick to point out her flaws. She needs to be knocked down a few pegs. Like that dancer who won the first-place overall high score three times in a row, kids can get cocky and start to think, "Why do I have to rehearse?" Sometimes I make the kid rehearse something on her bad side in front of everyone on the spot. I have been known to call on her to tell me the proper term for a dance step. And if she happens to get lucky naming the correct ballet step, I make her spell it. Ha ha! You want to make her look like a jerk in front of her peers to bring her back to reality. This is where the tough love comes into play. We are not dealing with novices. I am training budding professionals.

I want my dancers to be fabulous, fierce, and famous. I also want them to be kind, humble, and confident enough to book the job, get the job, and keep the job. I want my dancers to be nice enough that others want to work with them again and again. Be humble!

. . . .

Dear Abby:

My daughter wants to quit dancing and play soccer instead, but her teacher and I believe she has great potential as a dancer. What would you suggest we do to encourage her to stick with dancing?

Is she a good soccer player? Does she have college scholarships lined up? Could she go pro? Or is the soccer thing just something that's happening with friends at school? Once you start something and sign up at the beginning of the year, you have to follow through till the end. Maybe let her play soccer and get kicked in the shins a few times and she'll wise up and won't want to do it again next year. However, don't stop the ballet classes. Keep her in at least some dance classes once or twice a week while she dabbles in soccer. Eventually she will come to her senses.

Abby
. . . .

LEAVE WHEN YOU'RE ON TOP

By leave when you're on top, I mean exit gracefully—don't beg for another chance, and don't make a spectacle of yourself or have a temper tantrum. Just exit stage left. Know when your parade has come to an end and when it's best for everyone concerned that you step out of a particular situation. Like the dancer whose mom has had one too many altercations with other people, you need to understand when it's time to get out.

Sometimes you and a studio don't see eye to eye. It happens. You want to make a graceful exit or they'll show you the door. Either way, it's not fun. There is *no* nice way to throw a kid out. I've only physically thrown one kid out in all my years of teaching. She was a short tenth grader who was vehemently jealous of Heather Snyder, a promising student in her class. Heather was and still is a gorgeous, talented dancer who looks an awful lot like Cindy Crawford. She became Miss Dance of Pennsylvania her senior year, then went on to be first runner-up at the Nationals in New York City. There was a producer in the audience who needed one more girl for the first national tour of *The Will Rogers Follies*. He messengered a contract over to the Marriott Marquis the next morning, and Heather's career began.

Heather never said a nasty word to anyone, but this girl was a potty mouth and called her the F word one day in class. I lost it. Nobody used to speak that way in my studio. I made her leave the premises immediately! Now remember—this was before there were cell phones, so the kid couldn't even call her parents for a ride! She had to wait outside the building in the cold. I don't know how she got home. She never took another dance class from me, and guess what she became? A dance teacher and a born-again studio owner! God help us all . . .

HOW TO TAKE ORDERS, HOW TO GIVE ORDERS, AND HOW TO ORDER ROOM SERVICE
by Mark Myars

How did I learn to take orders? Well, that's easy . . . Abby Lee was my dance teacher. Enough said, right? I learned how to *give* orders when Abby asked me to be a class assistant and eventually an instructor at the studio. But it's how I learned to order room service that I'll cherish the most.

During my teenage summers, the senior company at the Abby Lee Dance Company would travel with Abby to New York City to attend national conventions and compete in national competitions. If you have ever been to Penn Hills, PA, you know that we are a hardworking, middle-class people, and if you have ever vacationed in the Big Apple, you know that New York hotels are outrageously priced. (Well, everything in New York is for that matter.) There were times when we would attend several conventions in one three-week stay, hopping from the Marriott Marquis to the Grand Hyatt to the Waldorf Astoria. How could we afford all of this? Well, we would cram ourselves, our dance bags, the girls' Caboodles, and our overpacked luggage and costumes into New York's tiny hotel rooms . . . and by "we" I mean up to twelve of us! We slept three to a bed; there were endless cots. We did whatever we had to do to make us all fit and stay under budget! We had rules to not get caught: Never take the elevator at the same time. Never make eye contact with hotel staff. And it was most imperative to leave the DO NOT DISTURB sign on the door at all times.

Now this may sound like complete mayhem to some, but we were teenagers from the 'Burgh in New York City! We took days of endless dance classes together. We taped one another's bloodied toes. We sweat with and on one another. We cheered one another to victory and took comfort in one another after defeat. We were inspired by Broadway! We ate at all the cool New York eateries (you know, like Hard Rock Cafe?). One night in our cramped room, after we'd packed up to move to the next hotel and she had finished dyeing her roots, Abby taught us how to order room service.

I have since moved to New York, and I've had a career full of ups and downs. Right now I am at a very "up" point. My dance supervising job has me traveling throughout the United States and around the world. I have had opportunities I never dreamed I could! However, when I'm in my hotel room biting into a cheeseburger that I just ordered from room service, I am at my proudest. I'm reminded of how Abby and the senior company helped me to get where I am today. I smile at the thought of all the memories we created together. Then I look around my hotel room and sigh, relieved that there are no Caboodles in sight.

Mark Myars is currently an associate choreographer on the Broadway musical *If/Then*. He is also the dance supervisor of *Wicked*'s Broadway cast, the North American touring companies, and the Japanese and Australian companies. He was the assistant choreographer of *Wicked*'s first national U.S. tour and of the productions in Chicago, Los Angeles, West End, Germany, Japan, and Australia. Mark has been seen on Broadway in *Footloose* (Original Dance Captain), *Wicked* (Original Dance Captain), *9 to 5: The Musical* (Original Dance Captain), *West Side Story* (Swing), and *Come Fly Away* (as "Marty"), as well as in the off-Broadway hit *Silence! The Musical* (as "Dream Hannibal"). Recently, he played "Mike" in Paper Mill Playhouse's acclaimed production of *A Chorus Line,* and he can be seen in the films *Center Stage, The Producers, Across the Universe, Rock of Ages,* and most recently *Winter's Tale*.

ABBY'S FAVORITES
There's More Than Just Maddie

- **Favorite quote:** "I don't know the key to success, but the key to failure is trying to please everyone else."
  —Bill Cosby

- **Favorite inspirational saying:** "Winning isn't everything, it's the only thing." —Henry Russell Sanders

- **Favorite epitaph:** "Will it matter that I was?"

- **Favorite dance:** Old-school lyrical.

- **Favorite Broadway show:** It's a five-way tie. The Abby goes to . . .
  - *Footloose* (a personal favorite because my first student to grace the Broadway stage was in the original cast).
  - *Priscilla Queen of the Desert* (I absolutely *love* the costuming!).
  - *Wicked* (because of my personal connection to Wayne Cilento).
  - Any Fosse show—because it's a Fosse show! (usually with John Kander).
  - *Whoopi Goldberg on Broadway* (a show that changed my life—it showed me just how powerful theater can be, and how I must choreograph poignant messages and controversial subject matter if I hope to make a difference in the world of dance competition).

- **Favorite song:** "Heard It from a Friend" by REO Speedwagon.

- **Favorite film:** *The Way We Were.*

- **Favorite color:** Like my mother I could never pick a favorite color, but I do have a great eye for color—I can look at an article of clothing, note the color, go to

Dillard's, and pick out twenty other things that match exactly. I'm good at that. Although I feel most confident in black, I guess my favorite color would have to be either red or hot pink.

- **Favorite meal:** Yum! I have lots of these. Chicken Parmesan with a side of fettuccini Alfredo at the Alcoma Country Club where I grew up. You got three pieces of chicken and the side on its own plate. I also enjoy a traditional turkey dinner with Stove Top stuffing, and I loved my mom's chili—it was so good.

I was a longtime member of Dance Masters of America (DMA) and I took it very seriously and dedicated my life to that organization, and they terminated my membership because of *Dance Moms*. When the show first started, it was very controversial because they filmed me making kids cry and focused on the negative instead of showing me in a positive light. They wanted that reality TV craziness, and all the dance teachers in the organization—who, by the way, were secretly so jealous they couldn't stand it—were up in arms because I was a part of their world and they were worried about how people would perceive dance instructors, assuming that all dance teachers were making their students cry.

Come on, *really*? Most of us have seen *Hell's Kitchen* on TV and we know that every chef isn't like Gordon Ramsay. We all know that Gordon Ramsay isn't really that mean in real life. It's a TV show!

DMA took up the best years of my life, or so I thought. I served on the board of DMA Pennsylvania Chapter #10 for four years, and as second vice president, first vice president, president, and naturally past president for two years in each of those offices. And I was an active member for many years after that. I didn't want to fight DMA because I didn't want to jeopardize my mother's and my faculty's memberships in the organization. I didn't have time for more chaos in my life. I had already given them my time, my energy, my heart, and my talent, not to mention all those winners who represented the organization so well. So heeding my own advice, I just wanted to exit gracefully. The good news is I can still state that I'm certified by test to teach by DMA. I received my twenty-five-year membership pin in 2011, when the show was filming its first six episodes. On the flip side, I'm proud to be a member of Dance Educators of America. Sometimes it's just better to leave when you're on top—they lost me, I didn't lose them!

Rarely do I have to tell a mom that her kid doesn't have what it takes. People are usually smart enough to take off the rose-colored glasses and realize that their child is not cut out for a professional career in the performing arts. *They* tell me before I tell *them*. We attend numerous conventions and competitions throughout the dance season. If your kid is *not* the big winner, the scholarship recipient, the one the instructors are talking to after the event, chances are nobody noticed your kid.

Clients leave my studio for two reasons and two reasons only: either they can't cut the mustard or they can't afford it. Usually if they can't afford it, they don't want to say they can't afford it—they're too embarrassed—so they make up other excuses to cover the financial issue, like they didn't like their costumes, or they didn't like their solos, or they didn't win, or they're always in the back of the group. Whatever they're upset about at the time, they vocalize it and make sure everybody else knows about it too. In the meantime, we know at the front desk that their parents' credit cards have bounced for the last three months and that the kids are embarrassed about it.

When you walk in and take my class but you haven't paid in a month, that's called theft by deception. You are taking the materials, you are taking education, but you're not paying. The tuition for my senior company, the most advanced group I have—which takes sixteen hours a week of dance instruction—is only $282.00 a month. If you break that down weekly, it's only $70.50 a week or $4.40 for an hour of dance instruction. I'm cheaper than a babysitter, and our prices have not gone up since the TV show.

Let's face it, if your kid shows real promise, you'll find the money somewhere, somehow. If you really can't afford the lessons, the costumes, and the entry fees, and you realize that there are other children who are better, then say so. Don't waste everyone's time and give your kid an inferiority complex. Just mosey off into the sunset. Happy trails.

ABBY'S ULTIMATE ADVICE
Three Key Points to Remember

1. Every dancer must constantly step up her level of performance just to stay where she is. Everyone's replaceable!

2. Dance instructors take their work seriously, and so must dance students. We are *not* babysitters!

3. Pull your own weight, be humble, and always do your very best.

THIRD POSITION
À LA SECONDE

Save Those Tears for Your Pillow

> Perfection is our goal, excellence will be tolerated.
> —J. Yahl

YOU ONLY CRY WHEN you break a bone or somebody dies. That's it. You think things are tough now? Just wait! Things are about to get a whole lot tougher. When Brooke, who happens to be the oldest girl in the group, wanted to leave rehearsal the day before a competition to go to a football game, and I said no, I could not believe it when she broke down in tears. There was the oldest girl on my team, looking like a six-year-old! Over a football game! News flash—the game will be played with or without you. If she thinks it's hard to miss a fun event with her friends, wait until it's time for her first Broadway rehearsal (LOL—we will be waiting a long time!), or she's cramming for four college finals at the same time, or her employer has some sort of issue with the work she's doing. Then she'll *really* want to cry, but she won't, because she's here training with me.

It's important to never let them see you sweat. Never back down. Never crack under pressure. Never shake in front of a casting director. Never crumble in front of a teacher or coach. Sure, when someone is dying or you're at a funeral, you should grieve. When you have a compound fracture and your arm is twisted, relocating your hand next to your elbow, then yeah, cry your eyes out!!! When you're putting an ice pack on your ankle and your ankle is triple the size it's supposed to be, weep to your heart's content. Otherwise, save those tears for your pillow. (Pillowcases available at abbyleedancecompany.com!)

Were you blessed with a child who's happy and healthy? Does he speak when spoken to? Does she mind her manners? *No?* Then you must be the parents of that little brat having a temper tantrum in the middle of the mall, the monster running round and round under the clothing racks in the department store, or perhaps the poor loser onstage making the judges and everyone in the audience feel a whole lot of uncomfortable. You see people looking your way, you get the dirty looks, and you hear the snide remarks. You know exactly what they are thinking—bad parenting; weak authority; they've lost all control and the kid's only six, just wait until he's sixteen.

If I come in contact with you at the department store in the mall, look out—I won't whisper under my breath. I have no problem yelling at *anybody's* kid—free of charge! Now, if you are part of my dance company and you step onstage for the award ceremony representing me, you better have a smile plastered on your face. I want to hear you say thank you from all the way out in my seat. You should have the common courtesy to mouth the words *thank you* to the judges down front. And you should always remember that you are *still onstage!* Everyone is still watching you. Keep your emotions in check. Did you think you were going to win? Did you think you had this one in the bag? Suddenly you find yourself accepting a second- or third-place plaque, then you hear the winner (your best friend's name) announced!

Your facial features change, you start to breathe a little heavier, and then the tears well up in your eyes. I'm watching, remember? Everyone's watching! And *now* you turn on the emotion? Really? Where was all that passion and honesty in your performance? Why are you showing everyone your true colors *now,* when it doesn't matter anymore?

When you cry because you didn't win, you look like a poor sport. You have to suck it up and put that smile back where it belongs. (A) You are representing me and the ALDC. (B) You may come across these judges again in your competition years—you don't want them to remember the kid who didn't win, but instead to remember the kid who should have won! I am training you to be a professional, so you must wait until you leave the venue, get back to your hotel room—alone with your mom—and then, and only then, sob into that pillow.

Abby Lee Apparel
"SAVE THOSE TEARS FOR YOUR PILLOW"

Nobody wants to be around a crying child. Have you been to Disney World lately? There are more kids screaming their heads off at the "Happiest Place on Earth" than anywhere else on the planet. Nobody wants to go to dinner at an expensive restaurant only to have a baby wailing away at the next table, especially when you made the effort to hire a babysitter for your kids so *you* could enjoy a romantic evening out.

Everybody wants to see a child happy and healthy. Then we have the nasty boo-hoo temper-tantrum crying, and certainly no one wants to see that. You see the looks when a child is acting out: people are calling the parents weak or idiots for putting up with the little brat who's behaving this way.

You have to remember that the girls on the show have a lot to deal with—being a member of the cast of *Dance Moms* is no piece of cake. The girls are rehearsing new numbers each week, listening to their moms yell at one another and watching them stab each other in the back—all while they're trying to just be normal kids. Each handles it a different way. Paige and Brooke are on their phones doing God knows what. Nia has always got her nose in a book. Mackenzie is doing a backflip and giggling, while Kendall is doing her makeup. Chloe is conspiring about something with her mom, and Maddie is watching dancers on YouTube.

The girls all have different ways of expressing their emotions. They have to learn how to deal with chaos because they have to use their feelings and emote during every performance. I've worked with all kinds of kids over the years: kids who are cold and who can't express themselves, kids who hold everything in and use the stage to show it, kids who have faces that tell a story, and kids who look clueless.

Then I have the kids who try to downplay their successes. We had that problem with Maddie in Season Three when she was winning and was very much downplaying each win. One time she received a crown when we hadn't even realized she'd been entered in the finals. When they placed the crown on her head, she took it off and gave it to the kid next to her to play with. The owners of the competition were probably thinking, "Here's Maddie, the star of a TV show, winning our competition, and we'll get all these pictures of her in this crown and put it all over our website." I can only imagine how they must have felt when she took off the crown and passed it off to someone next to her! Turns out she didn't want the other kids in our group or their moms to be mad about another victory—not mad at her necessarily but angry with her mom. She was worried they would treat her mom badly. She later told me that all that was going on in her head while she was out there trying to dance. Not knowing this ahead of time, I flipped out on her: "There are two hundred kids sitting behind you that would have cut off their right arm to get that crown on their head." And it's true.

My students participate in dance competitions because it's their opportunity to get onstage and perform. Years ago they didn't have competitions; they just put on shows. My mother, Maryen Lorrain McKay, owned and operated several dance studios in Miami, Florida, long before I was born. From 1945 through the early 1960s. Her students performed in the best hotels up and down South Beach. Her teen queens were employed as backup dancers for Sammy Davis Jr. and Dean Martin. Even her small-fries performed for the children who accompanied their parents to Florida for the winter holidays. They may have been paid in stuffed animals and toys, but they still got paid.

Nowadays, it's all about competition. Look at how many TV shows we have that pit people against one another: *American Idol, The Voice, The X-Factor, Dancing with the Stars.* Come on: wise up! These days, criticism comes with the territory. You have to have some pretty tough skin just to survive.

. . . .

Dear Abby:
Many of the girls on my daughter's team are getting frustrated because there is one particular student who never keeps up with the choreography. What can we do to help the girls deal with this frustration?

The ability to comprehend dance movement quickly is an asset to every professional dancer. However, this decision, this frustration, this problem is up to the dance teacher—not the moms, and not the other girls. If this child who's screwing up the choreography is causing them to lose competitions, the teacher will address it, fix it, and possibly lose a student—losing tuition money—but that's the way the cookie crumbles.

Abby

. . . .

THERE'S NO SUCH THING AS "OBJECTIVE"

Seriously—sometimes I have to question what judges are thinking when they award points. There's no rhyme or reason to it. It's whether they like you or not. Sometimes they don't like the song or the costume or even the makeup. Go figure. Sometimes I'll create a dance routine that I just love. I don't care what anybody thinks of it, because I believe in it. If we don't win, fine, I'm okay with that. That's the way it is: the people calling the shots get to choose who wins and who loses. When you try to succeed in life, you're just putting yourself out there, heart and soul open, to be judged, and you have to be ready to accept all criticisms, even when you don't agree with them.

Judges *always* have an opinion. They could hate the color red, hate the song "The Rose," or their pet peeve could be a dancer rolling around on the floor in a lyrical dance. It's their opinion, and they have been hired to give their expert opinion of you and to write down a score. There's no such thing as complete objectivity when it comes to scoring a dance performance. Sometimes the determining factor in a score can be who went before you or after you. There could be a dancer before you who gives a terrible performance and the judges increase your score because your performance looks better in comparison. The problem is that if you follow a bad dancer, but then more great dancers perform hours after you, you may end up with second or third place because the judges were basing your score on the low score ahead of you. It is actually better to follow the performance of a great dancer than a really bad dancer, so your score is higher if you outperform the great dancer before you. It's probability and statistics. See, I really am concerned with education.

It's all relative and based on who a judge sees perform next. A judge may give you a 98 and you think you've done amazingly well and the judge loves you, but then you realize that the judge is just a high scorer who gives everyone a 98. It's the kid who gets the 100 from her who wins. It's a numbers game, back to the math again. And you thought dancers only had to count to eight.

Another thing about dance judging and competitions is that scores are not posted right away as in sports like ice-skating. The teacher picks up the scores later. The judges know who won, but nobody else does. So if you win, you don't know if you won by ten points or by two-tenths of a point. Sometimes the judges will give a high score for the entire day of the competition, and that's a big deal. Like when Maddie wins highest score for the day after competing against sixteen- to eighteen-year-olds. That's huge, because Maddie is only eleven!

. . . .

Dear Abby:
My son dances in the house all the time and really wants to
dance, but he has a learning disability. How do we find the
right dance studio for him?

I strongly believe in checking out all the dance studios in your area, or because it's a boy, a little out of your area. Not everyone in the neighborhood needs to know what he's doing on Saturday afternoon. He should have the freedom and confidence to follow his dreams without others judging. Regarding the learning disability, I've had kids who were dyslexic and they shine as dancers, because when they look in the mirror, everything makes perfect sense to them. If it's a slow learner or perhaps some type of ADD, you never know. In dance class, learning is very different from academic classes that require books. They might pick up things quickly and that might be the way to go. Maybe that's their outlet, how they emote and get through the day. I would give it a try, but I wouldn't go in saying he has a learning disability, because that's just as bad as walking in and saying he's the next Mikhail Baryshnikov. Parents shouldn't do that either.

Abby

. . . .

ABBY'S BLOND BOMBSHELL
by Koree Kurkowski

Abby has always been someone I looked up to, listened to, and of course took correction from. She was the adult figure in my life who taught me a craft that has been my passion since the age of five. I continued dancing after graduation and I am still performing daily. A few years after leaving the studio and while I was dancing professionally in Las Vegas, Abby came to visit. We reunited with hugs and stories. I decided to give her the Vegas treatment and buy her a martini. One martini somehow led to another. By the end of the night, I was doing ballet barre at the bar! I thought I wasn't a student anymore. I guess I was wrong! It was a good experience seeing Abby let down her guard and have some fun. At the end of the night we went to her room to order room service. Abby fell asleep pretty quickly, but no worries—I enjoyed the famous fried rice from the Mirage by myself before heading home.

Koree Kurkowski fell in love with dancing at age five. She danced competitively with Abby Lee during her school years, then signed with Royal Caribbean while a senior in high school and performed for about two years with Royal Caribbean and Celebrity cruise lines. She moved to Las Vegas at age twenty after being hired as a showgirl/dancer in *Jubilee!* ("I was the shortest in the show at that time.") Other Las Vegas credits include *Pin Up, Sin City Kitties, Bite,* and *Fantasy.*

MAN UP!

When your kid is on the firing line, will she crash and burn? This is one of the reasons I'm so tough on my students. I would prefer for them to cry in front of me, their mentor, in the safety of the studio, not at an audition, baseball tryout, or ROTC boot camp in front of four hundred of their peers. When you walk into my classroom, I'm going to give it to you straight, just like in the real world, because that's the only way to prepare you for the real world. Part of my job is correcting flaws. It needs to happen. Better me than the first person auditioning you for a Broadway show, interviewing you for a job, or evaluating you for a promotion.

Showing a range of emotions onstage in a lyrical performance is wonderful. Performers taking on roles such as Helen Keller or Lizzie Borden require a range of emotions teetering on hysteria. These routines are what we call tearjerkers. It's great to be so expressive that you make the audience feel your pain or bring them to tears.

Offstage don't sweat the small stuff and get so worked up about every little thing. My mom was always rattled about one thing or another. Relax.

If you've been in my class for years, then you know that sometimes I come in and I'm in a rotten mood. It is a teacher's job to leave her troubles on the doorstep. The dance studio should be a place to set your spirit free, to forget your problems and just dance like nobody's watching. Then again, you've seen the moms I have to deal with, so let it roll off your back. You know I love you. Don't tell me your knees are black and blue, and then never wear knee pads or complain because your mother won't buy them for you. If you carried your sled up a hill of snow ten times and now your calves are killing you, don't come to me complaining about how sore you are. And don't tell me your legs are sore from dance class when I know what the curriculum is and I know there is no way your legs could be sore from dance class.

The parents at the studio think I'm a big ogre. They want to coddle and hug their kids, and shelter them from the big meanie. They tell their kids that *I'm* wrong and *they're* perfect the way they are. I tell the parents that if they want to save their kids from me, take them somewhere else. The parents and the kids know what they signed up for. They've been there since they were two years old. The studio was fine when they were three and four, five and six, and even seven and eight. Then the show started. They were happy customers until they had a little money and a little power. Then they became complainers. I am actually nicer on camera than I normally am, because there are things you just can't say on TV. I would never say anything racially offensive, but I would say, "This is a black piece. It's about Katherine Dunham," or I might say, "You need to feel like you're in that cotton field and you're carrying that basket."

I have a lot of male dancers and I'll tell them, "You look like a woman," or I'll say, "What do you think you're doing? Britney Spears doesn't want ten androgynous guys dancing behind her—she wants *men!*" I can't make comments like this on TV, because viewers will say I'm homophobic. Of course I'm not. In reality, my male students wouldn't be where they are today if they danced like girls. These men have to lift female performers and make them look pretty. This is how I normally speak to my students, but on TV, I can never say those things.

My mom and dad were older than the norm when they had me. So they raised me to be independent because they didn't know how long they'd be around. My dad, George L. Miller, died a horrible death from esophageal cancer on Father's Day in 2000. My mom, Maryen Lorrain Miller, passed away while I was working on this book, February 8, 2014. I think parents today do way too much for their kids. They forget that one day they're not going to be there and their kids are going to have to function on their own. Some parents do everything for their children—from doing their homework for them or, at the very least, writing a note to the teacher letting him know that they were up late the night before and didn't get their homework finished. Or if the kid doesn't want to go to Susie's party, Mom calls and makes excuses for the kid instead of giving the kid the phone and saying, "You call Susie and tell her you're not going to her party." Now, *my* parents would have insisted I go to Susie's party because we had already RSVP'd and bought her a gift. Parents tend to handle everything for their kids—they become their assistants. They let them get away with too much, instead of having their kids man up, face issues head-on, and deal with their own problems.

If my daughter came home and said she wanted a solo, I would make her go ask the dance teacher herself. If a mother calls me asking me if her daughter can have a solo, I'll tell her a hundred reasons why she can't have a solo. I want the kid to come to me, not the parent. I believe in throwing the kid into the pool, maybe with water wings, but throw him in. If you're afraid of letting a kid fly on a plane by himself when he's fourteen, then buy a plane ticket and follow him. Be fifty feet behind that kid, but let him do it himself and see how he does from a distance.

Have you raised your kids to survive on their own or are you doing everything in your power to keep this world a safe place for them where no one will ever call them a name, and no one is going to pull the chair out from under them, and no one is ever going to beep at them on the highway? I'll ask a student a question in the studio and the parent will blurt out the answer! When that happens, I say, "If she's merging onto the 405, and I'm behind her on the freeway entrance ramp and my horn is going full blast, is Daddy going to run out and stop traffic so she can merge onto the freeway?" No! Let your kids figure it out now! Train them now and force them to man up!

BUMPS, BRUISES, AND BREAKS HAPPEN

Dancers and athletes especially will fall, get whacked on the head, twist, sprain, and fracture things. I know moms want to kiss away every boo-boo, but that's not what your kid needs. In life, your first literal or metaphorical tumble won't be your last. And usually your ego hurts more than your injury.

Bumps, bruises, and breaks happen! You're enrolling in a physical activity where injury is likely to occur. It's very important when choosing a studio and the right teacher to find out what the floors are made of. Are the ceilings high enough? Is the studio a safe environment? Are there poles your kid might run into? All these things and more go into injury prevention.

Some kids are built stronger than others. Some kids have thicker skin than others. Is your child mentally and physically prepared for this activity? There will be bruises to her ego and hurt feelings. She will most likely have girlfriend issues. The old clichés "Two's company, three's a crowd" or "She's a fifth wheel" can play a role.

Girls can be really cruel. Sometimes the reason your daughter may not want to go to dance class is because of mean girls.

If your daughter is dancing for recreational purposes and coming to dance class only once a week for fun, there shouldn't be any injuries. If she's coming two or three days a week and she's involved, there might be an accident here or there. If there is core training, and your kid is training on cement or tile floors four or five days a week, you will have a problem. That's why it's so important to take a look at the floors before signing your daughter up for dance classes. Go to a facility that has special shock-absorbing floors designed for dance.

Your kid's feet are going to have a problem if you purchase cheap pointe shoes online instead of listening to your child's teacher and buying the right pointe shoes, which include a proper fitting.

It's important that your kid receives proper technical training that's even on the right and left side of her body. During a normal classroom session, your kid should be working both sides of her body to keep her alignment even.

If your body is telling you it hurts, then you need to stop and rest. If it's just one part of your body, then rest that part of your body, but just because you have to rest that part of your body doesn't mean everything else can't continue to work. If your daughter has a sprained ankle, she can still walk on her hands. She can still do elbow stands or chin stands in acrobatic class. She can still get her body into a split. As long as she isn't putting pressure on that ankle, she's okay. She can lie on her back and elevate her feet up in the air to do a hundred sit-ups every hour. She can get in a push-up position and put the sore foot up across the other foot behind the ankle and do push-ups with one foot.

If a kid is truly sick with pneumonia or chicken pox, she can't get all sweaty and gross in dance class. But she can lie in bed and watch old Gene Kelly or Fred Astaire movies and a *Dance Moms* marathon. She can study. She can read dance books and work on their terminology and vocabulary. She can continue learning to be a better dancer, even when she's sick.

You don't want to "work through the pain" with children because it can cause irreversible damage to their bodies. But you don't want to coddle them either. You want to acknowledge that your child is hurt—her right knee is bruised or twisted, or she tore her cartilage and has to go to therapy. But in the meantime, you want to point out to your child that there's nothing wrong with her *left* knee. You want to deal with and address the pain by seeing your child's doctor and getting an opinion, but you want her to continue to train the rest of her body. Some kids are so tight that they can lose their flexibility in just a month.

. . . .

Dear Abby:

For the most part, all the moms at our dance studio are very helpful and supportive, but we have one mom who gossips and spreads rumors about our girls and some of their parents. How can we put a stop to this?

One bad apple can spoil the whole bunch. Do not let this woman affect your child's education. You can decide to take the high road; be the better person and don't say anything at all. What goes around comes around. Let the gossip gods take care of her.

Abby

. . . .

OH, GROW UP!

They say patience is a virtue. I'm not so sure. Am I supposed to have patience with the kids? Yes, I'm a teacher, and that's my job. But patience with the parents? I just don't have time. Every moment I spend explaining myself, and the method to my madness, takes away from the time that I spend teaching their children. They don't understand me, nor do they care when it comes to competition. They like to take credit for their children's success. Never will they admit that I'm right. They want all the glory with none of the work!

Every child peaks at a different age. Some win every single competition before they are twelve, and then they crash and burn. Others might work and work and work and never win one title. But in the long run, all the sweat equity they put in over the years prepared them for the professional world, including the rejection. You can't predict the future and force it to happen. Yet parents still feel the need to call me and tell me how to do my job. And I warn you, telling any dance teacher how to teach is definitely setting your kid up for failure. I get that you're emotionally invested and that you don't like to see your child upset or disappointed. But it won't kill her, I promise you. It will make her stronger, more hungry for the win. No matter how much money you pay, or how many times you drive your kid to a dance class, ultimately your child is the one who has to get out on that stage and compete all by herself. Protecting her is hurting her. If your kid truly has what it takes, she will do it. She was destined to be onstage. And if she doesn't, she will enjoy a wonderful dance education anyway.

I admit there may have been one or two situations when a mom has made a good point or brought something to my attention that I was unaware of. But for the most part, I think kids handle competition much better than their parents do. Have you noticed? The kids are not usually the ones crying, screaming, and throwing tantrums.

So here's some advice: stop acting like a spoiled little brat. The "Mommy, I want it now" behavior is unbecoming. When kids come to an audition after being lazy and sitting on their butts all summer long, do they *really* think that they're the best? Do they *really* think they're going to be what I'm looking for? No! Even though I never had children of my own, I have raised hundreds of other people's kids. These kids need to figure it out for themselves. Be wiser and make better choices. Kids must learn that they can't improve if they miss classes, rehearsals, and workshops.

Years ago, dance studios were more like glorified babysitters, where people dropped their kids off and went to the mall, or home to make dinner and clean their houses. Now parents have time to stay. They want to watch, critique, gossip, have their noses in everything. They're living vicariously through their kids. I don't think they want to be their kids, they just want to provide their offspring with everything they didn't have when they were children. In some cases, they did try to excel, but it didn't work out well. Now they're just married with kids, living in the burbs and realizing they "never made it." Maybe they wanted to be a star when they were young. Who knows? I feel like a lot of these parents don't want their kids to grow up; they want to keep them little so they can continue to mold them.

My dad told me every day that I was dumb enough to be a twin. I think he meant I was dim enough for two people. I guess I must've been a beautiful baby because my parents didn't feel the need to constantly tell me that I was beautiful, but everyone else did. I hear these mothers telling their kids they are so pretty over and over, all day, every day. Don't get me wrong; in this business, pretty helps. Dancers from around the world audition for me and attend my master classes. There are some angelic faces that light up the room. There are kids so stunning the cameraman focuses on them. And then there are those exotic, interesting looks that capture your attention too. I can easily spot a child with the right *look*. Parents, be careful. Don't you want your child to be more than just another pretty face? Don't you want her to have a brain, personality, and talent? Be very careful that she doesn't rely on her looks to get her through life. It's nice when doors open easily but substance is important once you're on the inside. And remember, pretty is only skin deep, ugly is to the bone.

Kids are less independent now than they were years ago. Before, we all rode our bikes to the store without helmets! We went out in the woods and knew to come home when the streetlights came on. Nobody had a cell phone back then—our parents didn't know our whereabouts 24-7 like they do today. And guess what? Most of us survived just fine—in fact, better than just fine.

The problem with kids today is that their parents do everything for them. I think they aren't going to be the nurses and doctors who give me my medicine in the old folks' home. They aren't going to be able to function on their own.

ARE YOU MOM ENOUGH?
Channeling Your Kid's Passion

Answer the questions below honestly to see if you are helping or hindering your child's talent. Then see how you rate.

1. Your daughter is always dancing around your house, singing into a hairbrush. You:

   A. Tell her to keep it down. The neighbors will complain.
   B. Hire Britney Spears's manager for her and move to L.A.
   C. Enroll her in some dance and voice lessons, so she can learn correctly.

2. Your child sees a cooking show on TV and decides she wants to make you a four-course dinner. You:

   A. Tell her you're on a diet.
   B. Call Rachael Ray—maybe she's available for private coaching?
   C. Supervise the oven and chopping but let her experiment and wow the family with a feast.

3. Your son loves baseball and says he wants to play in the big leagues one day. You:

   A. Offer to take him to a Pittsburgh Pirates game so he can see how far he has to go.
   B. Sign him up to play with a league—and bribe the coach to show him some special attention.
   C. Get him a glove, ball, and bat and take him out in the backyard to practice.

4. Your daughter is obsessed with cutting her Barbie's hair. You:

   A. Refuse to buy her another doll unless she stops butchering the ones she has.
   B. Suggest she practice instead on real live models—maybe her BFF needs a new 'do?
   C. Take her to a salon and let her watch how stylists really cut and color hair.

5. Your eight-year-old is always standing on her head and tumbling around the house. You:

   A. Tell her to stop those shenanigans: all that blood rushing to her head is going to give her a headache!
   B. Contact Cirque du Soleil and ask if they need any able-bodied assistants.
   C. Sign her up for gymnastics classes so she can learn proper technique.

If you answered mostly As:
Bah, humbug! You are raining on your kid's parade! Don't pooh-pooh what he/she loves to do. Pay attention and try to encourage him/her more.

If you answered mostly Bs:
You've got *stage mom* written all over you. You push way too hard. Support your kid's interest but don't overdo it.

If you answered mostly Cs:
I like your attitude. You nurture your child's passion and help him/her get the lessons/skills needed to succeed. Maybe you can teach my dance moms a thing or two . . .

ABBY'S ULTIMATE ADVICE
Three Key Points to Remember

1. No one wants to hear your kids cry, least of all their coach, their teammates, and the judges!

2. Raise your kids to survive on their own—require them to man up!

3. Tell your kids to stop acting like a baby—the tears, the crying, the temper tantrums, and the spoiled little brat syndrome! Teach them to maturely make better choices.

FOURTH POSITION
ÉPAULÉ

Mother Doesn't Always Know Best

The best revenge is massive success.
—*Frank Sinatra*

MOTHER DOESN'T ALWAYS KNOW BEST, because Mother doesn't really know anything at all. For example, if a kid is into baseball, I really doubt that Mother came up through the minors into the majors. As for dance, I doubt most mothers ever go to New York City and see every new show with the original cast or dance with a major ballet company.

Every once in a while, you do get a mother who obviously knows about a certain activity and can critique and direct her child. There's a little girl who came to our classes in Atlanta. She is Daniela Silivas's daughter. Daniela is a former Olympic gymnast who received six Olympic medals. Her little girl is a budding gymnast too. Now if she wants to tell her daughter what she's doing wrong, this mom has every right. She also has the knowledge, the talent, and the experience to give pointers.

For the most part, though, mothers don't always know the best advice. They may *think* they know everything, but they may not know *anything*! They want their children to look up to them and to respect them, but mothers don't always know what they're talking about.

When it comes to my teaching, I don't want any discrepancies and I really don't want any opinions. I tolerate my dance moms best when they keep their mouths shut and don't say anything to me. I'm the teacher, it's my dance company, everyone plays by my rules, and I'm sure all the qualified experts out there in other fields feel the same way I do. Stay out of our business. I don't tell you how to perform a craniotomy, don't tell me how to teach dance.

Still, there always seem to be moms who just cannot control themselves. When I auditioned to fill a spot on our team, I was scouting for a very particular look. One girl, Payton, was simply too tall and too mature to fit in with this particular group of dancers. When I cut her at the audition, her mother had an over-the-top meltdown, screaming at me with her finger in my face in my own studio. What did this do for Payton? Not much. And will I ever send her out on a professional audition with a mother like that? Nope. Not gonna happen. So this mom sabotaged her kid's chances of success, simply because she couldn't zip her lip.

I would never go into a doctor's office, a school, or your husband's workplace and tell them how to run their business or how to do their job, so don't come into my dance studio and tell me how to run mine. This is not my first trip to the rodeo. I have found that if I give an inch, you will take a mile.

Sometimes mothers can't handle it when kids get into their teenage years and begin to confide in me more than they do their moms. Moms have a hard time handling that their children care more about what their coaches, teachers, or dance instructors have to say than what their moms have to say. A mom thinks she knows what's best for her family, when in fact she may know very little about organized sports, the game of golf, or Bach's concertos.

DANCE MOMS—THE INSIDE SCOOP!

As you've probably noticed by watching the show *Dance Moms,* those women can really drive me crazy sometimes. I'm not worried about them reading this book; they can't even read the ALDC rules and regulations handbook. They just can't seem to follow the rules, no matter how much they try. They are all vastly different, yet they have one thing in common: zero talent. Oh, yeah, and one more thing: they're all jealous of Maddie.

- **Melissa, a.k.a. Miss Congeniality.** She wants to be everybody's friend and always be in charge. She has to run it—that's her thing.

- **Holly, a.k.a. the Politician.** Oh so politically correct, but oh so wrong!

- **Jill, a.k.a. Forever Young.** Not only living vicariously through her daughters, she's wearing their clothes too!

- **Christi, a.k.a. the Mean Girl.** She's clawing her way to the top—one meet and greet at a time.

- **Kelly, a.k.a. Coulda, Shoulda, Woulda.** But now it's too late.

Believe it or not, the moms are worse off camera than they are on. You cannot believe how they've gone from rags to riches, and from bags to Botox, with this television show. My dad used to say, "It's like putting silk stockings on a mule," and in Christi's case, this definitely rings true.

I feel that the moms on a whole are very ungrateful to John Corella, who created the show with me and the Abby Lee Dance Company in mind, as well as to God above for putting them in the right place (registered at my studio) at the right time competing with the Abby Lee Dance Company (when they met John for the first time).

What nobody realizes is that the show came about when the Abby Lee Dance Company was on a trip to a national competition in Las Vegas. John was there too, and he came to the hotel to meet me. He hung out and

met all the moms sipping their cocktails at the pool of
the Alexis Park Hotel, which is an inexpensive place
far away from the Strip and all that some Pittsburgh
families could afford. At that time he was already
working on the idea for the show. Years later, after all
this crazy success with the show, he found himself
once again in the presence of a screaming lunatic. With
tongue in cheek, he reminded Christi, "Don't forget—I
met you when you were broke and drunk at the Alexis
Park Hotel!"

A couple of the moms think *they* made this
opportunity happen, that they had something to do
with creating a television show. They never stop and
reflect on the possibility that if it weren't them, it
would have undoubtedly been some other mother.
Most of the moms have class and self-control. They are
nice and polite in conversing with the other parents at
my studio. They are very good to my faculty members
and consider themselves part of the ALDC family. But
there are two who think they are higher and mightier
than everybody else.

Jill always had a little money, and she knows how
to act. Holly was raised with class and dignity and to
read books. Her sister is an attorney, her mother is a
judge, and her dad was a schoolteacher in the Bronx.
She is a good person. Melissa came from nothing but
she's on the ball. She's a go-getter with honey—sweet
and helpful.

. . . .

Dear Abby:

We live in a very small town with only one dance studio and my daughter really loves dancing there. The problem is, we feel that the dance teacher is not helping the girls reach their full potential—they never win a competition! Do you have any suggestions to help this studio create winning dancers?

What about the next town over? Keep your daughter where she is—don't bite your nose off to spite your face—but go to the next town or three towns over—up to ninety minutes away—to see if there's another studio that your daughter could attend once a week to get better training to improve her technique. Then perhaps tell the dance teacher or ask nicely and respectfully if your daughter can just do a solo at the competitions and not be in the group dances. If you see your daughter start to win on her own while the group remains stagnant, then, when the time is right and you're willing to drive those hours, you might want to make a switch. But please refrain from telling someone how to run her business. She doesn't really care.

Abby

. . . .

DON'T OVERSTEP YOUR BOUNDARIES

A good example of overstepping boundaries would be if I were to ask one of the moms at my studio to order rhinestones for the girls' costumes using my account with a wholesaler, and then at a later date she calls using my name to order rhinestones at wholesale prices for herself to use on her kid's dance bags, leotards, and costumes. That's overstepping the boundary—especially when she easily could have called one of my two stores and purchased rhinestones the retail way. I have a mercantile license and I pay sales tax, insurance and telephone bills, and credit card fees.

And it's not always the moms who overstep boundaries. One time a photographer who has a kid who dances at my studio needed a headshot of another student quickly, so I let him come in and get the shot. The kid's mother paid the photographer for his services. The next thing I know this photographer is taking more kids' headshots in my studio because he used that one kid's headshot as an advertisement. He was claiming to be Abby Lee Miller's official photographer. By the time I figured this out, he had already taken a hundred headshots, and a hundred kids' families had spent a fortune. I've got nothing to do with this photographer, and if it hadn't been for my allowing him to take that one headshot, he never would have had the opportunity to photograph all my students, resulting in all that money. That's overstepping your boundaries.

Here's another example. When students have been dancing with me from a very young age, once they turn eleven or twelve I have them help the younger students as class demonstrators. Then when they're around fifteen or sixteen, they become more like assistant teachers. When they're eighteen, and it's their senior year, I give them the opportunity to teach my curriculum. Every month they get a paycheck and they get a lesson plan from me for their next month of classes. A teenager is overstepping her boundaries when she starts teaching dance lessons to neighborhood kids in her basement, or she has a dance room in her house above the garage and she's charging money for youngsters in the area to come take dance lessons using my curriculum, my lesson plans, and my accumulated knowledge. That's overstepping your boundaries. Don't do it!

. . . .

Dear Abby:

There is one student in our studio who is very disruptive during classes—making excessive noise, blurting out rude comments, and acting bored. It seems as if the teacher isn't sure how to deal with her rude behavior. What would you suggest?

The dance teacher could be a wonderful woman with excellent training. However, she doesn't have the ability or the teaching credentials to deal with a student who obviously is crying out for attention. I've had students in my class do this very same thing. They want to hear their name whether it's good or bad, and whether they're being praised or scolded, it doesn't matter. Something is going on at home and that kid is starving for someone to pay her some attention. So look the other way. Tell your own child to ignore the situation and concentrate on her lessons.

Abby

. . . .

PATIENCE IS A VIRTUE

So often, people want instant success, instant glory, instant applause—they don't understand that you have to work for many years to become great at something. I believe that with any sport, including the performing arts, like dance, ballet, and tap, it's a very long process. Stop looking for a huge improvement overnight.

Oddly enough, I don't have that many pushy parents. I always have to be the pushiest stage mother with my students, more so than any parent. In fact, I am Queen Stage Mom. In New York some of my friends call me Mama Rose, after infamous Gypsy Rose Lee and her mother! I wear that label proudly. I'm going to get the best for my kids, make the most out of it, get them every opportunity, and knock down the doors until those kids are famous.

In the past I've had stage mothers at our studio try to outsmart me. Moms take their little lasses behind my back to study elsewhere or to learn a new trick at another studio. They don't understand that I'm going to find out about it and it's going to backfire on them, or that the kids can get hurt by being taught something they aren't ready to do yet, which is why I didn't teach it to them myself. I think these parents are trying to impress me and they go about it in the wrong way instead of through their kids' due diligence and hard work and being exemplary students.

That would impress me more. I'll give opportunities to the kids if the opportunities are right for them. I would never send your kid to an audition that she can't handle. If it's an ethnic call, and your spitfire has red hair and freckles, she's not going to the audition. It's a waste of everyone's time and money. If they are seeking advanced dancers who tumble both right and left, I've done my research, I know the choreographer, and I'm sure your kids can't handle it. Trust this is not because I don't like your kids; it's because they just aren't right for this opportunity. At least not right now.

In the gym, you can observe one gymnast training every day to learn a back tuck, which is a rotating somersault in the air traveling backward. She's spotted by her coach but just can't seem to get it—she keeps working hard and is still not setting high enough or is landing too short, falling to her knees. Then all of a sudden the day comes when she completes a successful back tuck. She runs down the mat, she preps, her round off is clean, the back handspring powerful, and, boom, a back tuck. She has successfully completed her first unassisted backward tumbling pass! She goes on to do it ten more times. It's instant, and she can do it again and again once she does it for the first time. For gymnasts, it seems like that day just comes, and one day they're just able to complete the stunt after trying for so long.

Ballet doesn't happen that way. Tap doesn't happen that way. Contemporary doesn't happen that way. Soccer doesn't happen that way. I think parents want their kid to wake up one day and be instantly good. It's the gratification of "My kid can do that." Most physical, technical refinement takes a lot longer. I feel like the slow-and-steady turtle wins the race when it comes to dance. Patience is definitely a virtue.

Many times I see boys take up dance later in life around their teenage years because they're tall and strong and can lift the girls. These boys don't learn the foundations of dance before they are thrown into senior company numbers. It's kind of like putting the tween in calculus before he has time to learn his multiplication tables. He walks into a studio, learns to lift girls, learns those big jumps and impressive turns that men usually do with years of extensive training, but he doesn't know the basics. This is a great example of patience as a virtue because these boys need to start at the beginning. They need to audit miniclasses and learn how to cross the floor properly and learn the basics of movement before they can attempt that solo. Instead, they are going to end up with injuries and poor technique. They're going to end up looking stupid in auditions when the casting person asks them to perform something specific and they have no idea what she's talking about. Learning proper terminology is key. Think beyond the world of competition. Do you have the knowledge to be the dance captain, the assistant choreographer, the dance supervisor?

. . . .

Dear Abby:

I am having a really hard time getting my eight-year-old daughter ready for dance practice. She drags her feet and says she doesn't want to go, yet when we get there, she has so much fun and always says how much she loves to dance. How can I make the transition from home to dance class easier? Is there a certain age when you just give up trying?

A lot of kids go through change: one year they love dance and the next, not so much. You say she drags her feet and doesn't want to go, but once she's in the room she loves it. Then don't go from home to dance class, go from school straight to dance class. Maybe her friends on the bus home are talking about watching TV or what game they're going to play that day or another activity they go to, whereas your daughter has to go to dance class. Or maybe someone at dance is giving her a hard time and she's not sharing the information with you. I would stick to your guns and make her go, because she's going to grow out of this phase and into another one.

As for the question of age, I don't think you should base your decision on a certain age, but instead on a certain level of talent. Does the kid really have talent? Did she invest years of sweat equity and sore muscles for her craft? Have you invested a lot of money and time as well? Have you been to enough competitions? Have you gone to real auditions? Have you taken her to L.A. and New York? Have you really done the utmost as the parent to see this through?

My advice? Don't let her quit. You don't know how

many kids I bump into at the mall whose names I don't even
remember, but they run up behind me and say, "Do you
remember me?" and the next thing they ask me is "Why did
my mother let me quit?" I think you need to really look at
each case individually.

Abby

· ·

ABBY'S BFF
by Colleen Johnson

Abby and I were destined to become best friends.
After all, when we were babies, our parents would place
us in the same playpen during their late-sixties soirees,
progressive dinner parties, and Super Bowl celebrations.
We actually attended separate elementary schools, but
were able to reconnect in high school in, of all things,
a cooking class, which we failed (not an easy thing to
do). Abby made high school fun and it seemed we never
stopped laughing. Come to think of it, maybe that had
something to do with the entire cooking class failing.
It seemed we were perfect for each other. She always
thought I was funnier than I actually am, and I always
found her incredibly entertaining. I'm glad she is finally
getting paid for her antics.

As you can imagine, Abby lives at the dance studio.
Every Friday night, I would go to the studio and pick
her up to go to the movies. She always wanted to drive.

I think it was because she preferred her Cadillac to my Ford Escort. Of course when I was with Abby I always had a job. On Friday nights, it was to sweep the bottom of her purse to try to salvage any crumbs of broken blush or powder that she could use to freshen her makeup as she was driving to Monroeville. Most people go to the movies and enjoy nice buttery popcorn as a snack. Not us. We would always drop by the local Italian restaurant in the mall and pick up the meatball platter, which we snuck into the theater with us. There were certainly quite a few turned heads once the movie began and we dug into our feast.

Shopping was of course a big part of our lives, and the midnight sales at Christmas were one of our favorite times. While we were searching the lot for a place to park, I was the designated spot saver. If Abby saw an open space anywhere, she would throw me out of the car so I could run to the empty, coveted space and pose until she could navigate her big boat in. Keep in mind, we grew up in Pittsburgh, and standing outside in an open parking lot in a polar vortex is not the most fun I've had. Abby loved to wear a full-length mink coat. (What teenager wears a full-length mink coat?!) We referred to Abby's coat as "The Beast." One night while shopping, Ab found herself too warm in her coat. Well, my job that night was to hold The Beast for the duration of our trip. I had no intention of carrying this thing through the stores, so I left it lying on the floor of the lingerie department. It was not until we were looking at shoes that Abby noticed that The Beast had gone missing. We just started laughing hysterically and found The Beast right where I had left it. I guess nobody else wanted to carry it around either.

I moved to Florida a few years after graduation. Abby would travel down to visit quite frequently. Every time she came, she would pack enough things for a month. On one particular visit, in addition to her giant, overweight luggage, she brought along a large duffel bag. Inside the duffel was a full week's supply of Nutrisystem products. This was the new diet that Abby was on, and she said that's all she was eating during the entire week. Well, the perfectly portioned, prepackaged, freeze-dried, diet delights remained untouched inside the duffel bag. When it came to the last day of her trip, the bulging duffle had never been unzipped (no surprise really). Abby did not want to take it all the way back to the 'Burgh with her, so on her last day, we decided to invite a few people over to my parents' house for a Nutrisystem smorgasbord. These prepared meals are designed to be eaten one meal per sitting. I will never forget Abby saying, "Hey, these things aren't too bad if you eat five or six of them."

Abby's dominant personality has been a constant during her entire life. She is always loud, and she's used to conducting class and being the center of attention because most other people bore her. We often referred

to her as Hurricane Abby when she arrived in Florida.
You can prepare all you want, but there's no telling what
the damage will be by the time she leaves. Don't worry
about southern hospitality with Abby. As long as you
have a bag of M&Ms and real Coca-Cola, she's a happy
camper. Even though we now live a thousand miles
away from each other, we've still remained buddies.
Now I get to see her every week—Tuesday nights at nine
on Lifetime.

Colleen Johnson grew up with Abby in Penn Hills and
remains one of her closest friends to this day.

PLAY NICE

By nice, I mean say please and thank you. Help out your
friend or your neighbor. If someone forgets her tights and
you have several new pairs, let her use an extra pair. If you
would like her to pay you back for the tights, tell her she
can pay you next week or she can pay you at the studio. And
don't talk about her behind her back for the next ten years
because she never paid you back—maybe she forgot. Let
others borrow your things, because someday your luggage
is going to get lost and you're going to need something.

Dancers have manners. They are considerate of
other dancers around them. It's called spatial awareness.
There is a certain etiquette that goes unspoken. A dancer
wouldn't go into the front or middle of a class as a guest. If

my kids went to New York City to Broadway Dance Center and walked in to take a class, they wouldn't go and stand in the front row, because those spots are for students who take the class every single day. Be respectful of the regular attendees, be conscious of your work space, and don't dance too big, bumping into people. This shows you're an amateur, not an advanced pupil. If you accidentally collide with someone, say, "I'm sorry," or "Excuse me." Work your way to the front of the class because you're that talented and you deserve to be there, but don't ever expect to start there. As the class progresses, perhaps the instructor will notice you and signal you to move forward.

Now when you're at an audition or master class, that's an entirely different situation. If you want to be noticed—and you do—then you can't be in the back drinking out of a water bottle. You have to get up front and impress them with how great you really are. You don't do this by pushing your way to the front. When you walk into a ballroom and there's a platform set up where the teacher's going to stand, you want to get yourself as close as possible. Put your dance bag and coat underneath a chair on the side of the room, and take your spot on the floor. If you aren't sure what the style is going to be like or how difficult the choreography will be to pick up, then you want to start in the middle. When you become more comfortable and confident, then work your way to the front.

When you're onstage and performing, there will be times when you have to wait in the wings, so use your manners backstage too. While you're waiting in the wings, stay calm and quiet. Jumping up and down could distract the person who is performing onstage. While waiting your turn to dance, you should always be alert and ready to make an entrance. Treat other people the way you want to be treated, and remember that if you're not nice, you may be seeing that person again and he or she might be the one hiring you for the job—or not.

I never knew this until many years later, but one of my blond bombshells was onstage in a major competition, dancing her heart out. As she approached the risky penché on relevé, another one of my students, her teammate and so-called friend, was doing everything she could to distract her focus and throw her off balance. It's all about the win, isn't it?

This goes both for children and for their parents. How is your child going to learn to be respectful of her peers if you trash-talk your fellow moms behind their backs? I'm amazed at how childishly some of my dance moms behave. I can honestly state that I never heard my mother say more than "damn" or "hell," and my dad was a "goddamn it" and "Jesus Christ" kind of guy. Probably just to tick off my devout Catholic mother. Ladies, your daughters are taking their cues from you! Is this what you want them to do? Is this how you want them to act when they're adults? My tongue is sharp, my quips are nasty, and my critiques are stinging, but I rarely swear and never at a child. The way these moms throw the

F word around, you'd think they were longshoremen who'd been out to sea for months on end. (No offense to the fishing industry.)

....

Dear Abby:

My daughter loves to dance, but she clearly has two left feet. She never wins during individual competitions, and at times I feel she is bringing her team down because she frequently forgets her choreography. Should I pull her out even though she loves to dance?

A child who loves to dance should be dancing, but maybe not competing. Isn't there a way she can go to a studio that does performances and puts on shows in the neighborhood or senior citizen homes and stuff like that where no one is judging, so she won't risk the loss for the rest of the team, and, most important, it doesn't hurt her self-esteem? Then she can just do it, have fun, and go out there and perform in an annual recital. That's what this experience does for your daughter.

Abby
....

STAND UP FOR YOURSELF

When a parent pokes her nose in, I want to slam the door on it. A child needs to understand that in life, you need to be your own advocate. You need to speak up if you believe in something strongly. I love it when a kid comes to me and says, "Hey, Miss Abby, I would really love a solo! I'll work hard. I won't let you down. I want to take a risk!" After Asia showed up on our team, Mackenzie was feeling like an afterthought (her "injury" didn't help matters—I'm not doubting the doctor's diagnosis, but the timing was suspect). We had an opportunity to perform on *The View*, and I had to choose between Asia and Mackenzie. I knew 'Kenzie was dying to be on *The View*, but I hadn't heard a peep out of her. Finally, she came to me and said, "Miss Abby, I'm ready to dance. Please let me do it." And that's why I chose her. Because she stood up for herself.

Mackenzie *was* ready, but lots of kids ask for things they are definitely *not* ready for. And lots of parents ask for lots of things their kids just aren't ready for. Jill is always nagging me to give Kendall a solo. I've never understood why on earth a parent would want to humiliate her child. Why would she not trust the teacher (whose knowledge she is paying for, right?) to choose who deserves a solo this week? Dancing around your living room is one thing; spending money to dance on a stage at a competition to get judged by professionals is something completely different. And I find it's always the same old scenario: The child with all the talent who would be an excellent ALDC member has been awarded to parents who aren't interested, can't afford it, or simply don't give a damn. The child with absolutely zero natural talent is usually blessed with overzealous parents who can't see past the rhinestones. They will pay for countless private lessons, they will persist, and they will wear you down until you start to see Precious Penelope through their eyes and eventually give in. Wouldn't you be better off to let *me* make the call? Let *me* teach Penny and put her onstage when she's ready to take home the overall high score solo place rather than fall flat on her face?

DANCE MOMS—THE INSIDE SCOOP!
On the Bus

I love all my dancers! A tyke toddles into the studio with a big pink bow in her hair the size of her head. She doesn't know her right foot from her left, but she knows I am her teacher. Together we will learn and love and lose and laugh. If all goes well, in approximately fifteen years that accomplished young protégée will walk out the door to begin a professional dance career and I can proudly put another feather in my cap. I really do always have my students' best interests at heart. I want them to discover that they can do far more than they ever imagined. Whether that means landing a job on Broadway, performing in a Las Vegas Cirque show, or touring with a pop star.

Here are my nicknames for my girls on *Dance Moms,*

and what they're usually up to while we're taking those long bus trips to competitions every weekend:

- **Magnificent Maddie.** Maddie is calm, cool, and collected. She's usually watching YouTube dance videos—or creating her own.

- **Party Paige.** Paige is fun and sweet, and always the life of the party. However, there are rules for a reason; you shouldn't be standing up on a bus that's going 65 miles an hour.

- **Brooding Brooke.** Brooke is either sleeping or slouching, and she loves to sing. I just wish she would take her ear buds out long enough to hear my roar.

- **Rock Star Mackenzie.** Mackenzie is very vocal. "Are we there yet? How much longer until we're there and when are we going to get off this bus?" She makes rubber bracelets, silly home movies, and typically wastes hours of her valuable time.

- **The Good Kid Nia.** Nia is always watching a movie, reading a book, or keeping Mackenzie in line.

- **Pretty and Impetuous Kendall.** Kendall is probably looking at herself in the mirror, putting on makeup, or shopping online.

• **Clever, Queenly Chloe.** Chloe is always with the tutor in the front of the bus. It seems like she monopolizes the tutor's time.

When the show initially started, all the girls were friends. There has never been an odd man out, but the way they pair up on the bus is quite interesting. Nia and Mackenzie are thick as thieves. Brooke, being the oldest, sits with Maddie, probably because they're boring. Chloe and Paige are silly blondes—there you have it.

I make my rules very clear on the bus. There is no clapping, snapping, or patty-caking. No screaming, shrieking, or loud giggling will be tolerated. Don't get me wrong. If something funny happens on that bus, we're all going to chuckle. But let me tell you, listening to a bus full of little girls giggling for five hours straight is going to grate on anyone's nerves. If we're in my car and I'm driving, that's a whole other set of rules.

The girls keep themselves busy on the bus. They have fun. They FaceTime. They make Video Stars. They play games. They even play cards. I wish they would use that time more wisely by working on their dance terminology and history and watching some classic dance movies. Sometimes the entire bus watches movies together, which is fine; you have to make the time pass quickly or you will all go insane.

The production crew sits in the front of the bus where it smells fresh and clean. The cast has to sit in the back, by the bathroom. When I was a kid all the cool kids sat in the back of the bus, but this is not a ski trip in high school with a hot guy. This is work, and I sit in the middle so I can yell at the bus driver, keep the crew in check, and keep an eye on each of the moms.

Speaking of the moms, here's what they're usually up to on the bus:

• **Holly** is either on the computer or reading.

• **Christi** is on the phone fighting with somebody, probably the production company about something.

• **Melissa** is loud and talky-talky to everyone on the bus, even when they're trying to sleep.

• **Kelly** is either screaming at her children or sleeping. But you can bet her feet are tucked up underneath her on the seat.

• **Jill** is sweet and looks in the mirror a lot, just like her daughter Kendall.

I've experienced all kinds of children in a wave. Many are sugar and spice and everything nice in the classroom, then somehow unbeknownst to me they turn into holy terrors telling tales outside of school! I thought the class went great and everyone got equal attention and their share of corrections. Nothing seemed out of the ordinary, until the little sweetie got Mom and Dad all fired up over something that happened, something that was said or something someone did to their oh-so-innocent child. The perfect parents have filled up my in-box with their nonsensical e-mails and used up all the voice mail space in my cell phone. And made complete fools of themselves on the studio's answering machine eleven times over. I expect them to barge into the studio screaming and yelling at me first, then at every other parent. Now, my old-school mom and dad would have never reacted in that manner. They would have told me to handle it; after all, it's my world and I have to live in it every day. It's up to the crybaby to take charge of the situation herself by saying something: "I don't really need to be your friend anymore," or "You're really nasty," or "I hear you keep talking about me. If you have something to say, say it to my face."

I think a lot of the fighting and bickering that happens between moms stems from their own kids. I have to blame the parents too. They should stop their kids from complaining to them about anything and everything dance related. When competition plays a key role in your child's activities, you are playing with fire. The dancer, athlete, or scholar should redirect her issues to her coach, choreographer, or professor. I don't claim to be a doctor of psychology but I do know kids. On occasion even the best kids need a little extra attention from Mom and Dad. They want to ensure that you have their back, that you would go to the ends of the earth to protect them. So when they raise a ruckus, they never ever conceive that whining to Mom and Dad would cause a chain reaction that gets them expelled from their dance school and thrown off the team. Be careful what you wish for!

Children need to be independent. They need to fight their own battles themselves because they're never going to learn if Mom and Dad try to fix every little thing. If a kid is a troublemaker and is starting problems—like the kid who thinks it's great fun to play other kids against each other in groups (and I've had many of those)—the mom and dad are usually completely unaware of it. They have this little con artist who is wise way beyond her years and they have no idea. They think their whippersnapper is clever like clover. She's actually a little devil and she's starting trouble and she's a constant problem. Attention parents: if your child is only eight and already marked with the scarlet letter, you're in for much bigger problems ahead.

I try to encourage my dancers to come to me and work out their problems instead of running to their parents. Often they don't even need to come to me and start a conversation or be verbal about it. They just need to show me in their will to work, show me in their technique, show me by arriving early and warming up and being ready to go as soon as class starts. This proves to me that they're eager beavers and they are going to nail this number. That way there's no need for a conversation or any drama.

Bottom line—don't fight all your kid's battles. If you allow yourself to get caught in the middle of that whole girlfriend thing by calling the other mother, you're going to look pretty ridiculous the next day when the kids are best friends again. Just let your kid figure it out on her own, live and learn, and laugh at it all.

ABBY'S ULTIMATE ADVICE
Three Key Points to Remember

1. Mother doesn't always know best. In fact, chances are your dance instructor knows a lot more about dance than you or your mother.

2. Be patient—when you're ready to progress, your instructor will take you to the next level.

3. Learn about theater etiquette. Say please and thank you. Help out your teammates. Be nice, but stand up for yourself when necessary.

When There's a Crown on Your Head, Someone's Always Watching

A girl should be two things: classy and fabulous.
—*Coco Chanel*

I AM A STICKLER for manners and etiquette. I don't understand why most parents are not. Your child is a representative of you, your family, and her upbringing. Did you raise her in a beautiful home in the suburbs or a barn?

The moment a crown is placed on your pretty little head, you must stand up straight! Instantly you are in the spotlight, and everybody's watching you. They examine your entrance, they study your stride, they observe the obvious. So you better not pick your nose, burp, slouch, put your elbows on the table, or try to eat all your meat at once without cutting it one piece at a time. You need to use the correct fork, pass the rolls in the right direction (counterclockwise), and be well-versed in appropriate topics for dinner conversation. In other words, when you teach your kid to say "Mama" and "Dada," the next words should be "please" and "thank you."

Nothing irks me more than a kid who acts like she's got something coming to her—that she's *entitled*. I am not your servant, and I deserve to be asked and answered with respect. If someone does something nice for you or gives you a gift, send a thank-you note *immediately*. Cross your ankles, put your hands in your lap, and be a good role model to everybody else. One more thing: you can't smoke, or drink, or swear when you're wearing a tiara on top.

Dance like nobody's watching. Stand like the world is at your feet.

. . . .

Dear Abby:
The studio my daughter dances at actually makes us request
vacation time well in advance, and then we can only take a
vacation if they approve it! This seems a bit extreme to me. Is
it normal for a dance studio to ask parents to put in a request
for a family vacation?

I really don't care when you go on vacation as long as
your daughter/son on my competition team is available
to rehearse and prepare for our national competition. You
and your husband don't have to go. The rest of the family
can stay home. You can go wherever you want, but that kid
better be with me. So, yes, the studio is right—when we
attend Nationals in New York City, Las Vegas, or Orlando,
we block all the summer dates. They should give you their
dates too that are not available for a family vacation. You

don't practice and prepare all year from September to June
only to get to July and have to rechoreograph all the routines
because someone decided to go to Ocean City, New Jersey.

Abby

. . . .

BEHIND THE SCENES
My Least Favorite Dance Moms *Moment*

In one episode, Maddie supposedly forgot her dance,
but in reality it was all set up by production. When I say
set up, I don't mean it was created—nothing is fake—I
mean they set a ball in motion at the beginning of the
week so that Maddie didn't have enough studio time
to finish learning her solo. Chloe had completed her
entire piece, and then we started Maddie's. We only got
through sixty-four counts and they said we had to leave,
get out of the studio, our time was up. I had a meeting to
go to, and I said to my assistant choreographer, Gianna,
"When you get back to the hotel, find some area, some
lobby or some space, and finish Maddie's number. You
don't go anywhere and she doesn't go anywhere until
that routine is perfected."

They got back to the hotel and Maddie and the rest
of the girls to go to dinner. The kids didn't get back until
11:00 P.M. By then my assistant, Gianna, was gone—an
ALDC alum wasn't going to sit around all those hours

waiting, while the Big Apple was ripe for picking. Melissa is a very go-to-bed-early, get-up-early kind of person, so she was out like a light. She has so much faith in Maddie, she didn't seem at all concerned about the solo. Unbeknownst to me, Maddie ended up learning the remaining two-thirds of the routine in the morning— the morning of the competition!

The other thing that you don't see in the episode is that the jib camera operator didn't know what he was doing, and during the competition we attended, two kids before Maddie and two kids after Maddie ran off the stage because they forgot their dances; three kids in ten minutes. That *never* happens.

That happened because the jib operator was swinging the camera down in front of their faces. Maddie came out of a turn and the camera was less than twelve inches from her face and she couldn't do the next step because she would have hit the camera. Then she forgot what she was doing. I think that was absolutely criminal on the part of the jib operator, the director, the producer, and all involved.

I know when she came off she was hysterical, and I don't want to ever see that happen to a kid, especially one who works so hard and usually carries my team to victory. A dancer who couldn't care less, never comes to rehearsal, misses technique classes, and goofs around is more likely to forget her dance. That's fate. You get what you deserve. But some artists deserve nothing but respect.

NO INTERRUPTIONS!

Never interrupt someone's thought process. Don't become the kid who always has to go to the bathroom in the middle of class. This also goes for the moms. Don't interrupt the teacher when she's teaching. When a mom interrupts dance class because her daughter needs a costume, she just throws everyone on the dance floor off track, including me. I may have had the next sixteen counts of brilliant choreography in my head, and now I can't even remember my name, because the mom threw me off track.

Am I speaking to someone else? Am I in the middle of a lesson? Then why are you talking out of turn? If I ask you something, answer it. Otherwise, listen and look and raise your hand if there's something pressing that can't wait. And it better not be "Can I go to the bathroom?" because that should be done before class, between classes, or after class!

When I'm talking to the girls, if I'm giving a speech or a lecture, don't interrupt me. If I'm explaining something about the costumes, how the straps get sewn, or what special makeup you need to purchase, don't interrupt me. Save your questions for the end because I'm probably going to answer your question by then anyway. If you listen long enough, I'm probably going to answer every question. I've been doing this for thirty-three years and I know what I'm doing. When a mom keeps interrupting, I make her offspring drop and give me twenty push-ups, although I would love to make the mother drop too.

If you are in class, at dinner in a restaurant, at a show or a movie, or anywhere where people are busy or enjoying themselves, shut off your phone. No ring; no vibrate; nada. Immerse yourself in the happenings around you. Engage the company you're with right here and now. I wish I had a nickel for every time I had to tell a kid to stop texting or playing games on her phone. Phones are a distraction, and if you're not old enough to understand phone etiquette, then you're not old enough to own one. That's the beauty of a phone: you can hang it up.

Phones have become tracking devices for your children. When I was young, we knew to look both ways before crossing the street, to ride our bikes on the side of the road, not in the middle of the street. We had money in our pockets for the ice cream truck and it was an unwritten law that you had to be home when the streetlights came on. When did this all change? You have got to let your children have some leeway. Why don't you trust them? Don't give me that old adage about trusting them but not the rest of the civilized population. You've got to give a kid enough rope to jump all by herself or you will catch her rappelling out of her bedroom window down the side of your house. Raise a pillar of the community not the neighborhood sneak.

A Star Is Born - Abigale Lee Miller
September 21, 1965

A Wonderful Childhood

ABIGALE L. MILLER

Because Abby Said!

abby lee DANCE COMPANY

Founded 1980

Rising Star '93

WELCOME! HOCTOR'S DANCE CARAVAN

ABBY LEE DANCE COMPANY

DANCE CARAVAN

RISING STAR

U.S. AIR

Dance Aquarius
Sail the Sea with Abby Lee

Brand New State-of-the-Art Facility
Maryen Lorrain Dance Studio
Home of the Abby Lee Dance Company

MASTER CLASSES
With Master Instructor Abby Lee
Official Abby Lee Apparel
Available at abbyleedancecompany.com

Abby Lee Dance Company
Takes a Bite out of the Big Apple

- -

Dear Abby:

I don't understand why after paying thousands of dollars a year for my son to dance at our local studio, the studio also requires parents to volunteer for chaperoning, costume alterations, fund-raising, makeup application, etc. We pay so much money already! Shouldn't the studio be providing these things?

I don't know where your studio is located, but costume tailors and professional makeup artists are not readily available in most small towns across the United States. Unless you're in the New York area or Chicago or Los Angeles, you won't find makeup artists who will come and be able very quickly to do two hundred and fifty kids' faces for a competition number or a show. Furthermore, you should want to be involved in your child's activities. You should volunteer to chaperone or do fund-raising because you want to be part of his hobby and special interest. One last thing, is your son attending classes on a scholarship? Because most boys at most studios are. Actually, I wonder if your child is getting things for free that the girls are paying a lot more for. In that case, you should definitely be there volunteering.

Abby

- -

ABBY'S STOLEN WALLET
by *Sandy Powers*

Over the course of the last thirty years I have shared many crazy experiences with my friend Abby, but the one that comes to mind first is an early spring weekend in New York City.

As always, Abby had a plan and she runs the show, so we had to squeeze the most out of every minute. First, a bagel on the street, and then we were off to the garment district. We trudged from one fabric store to the next, with Abby barking orders to the shopkeepers and workers scurrying around cutting her fabric. There was no time to waste because we had matinee tickets to a Broadway show.

While racing down the street to grab a quick lunch before the theater, a gentleman bumped into Abby and kept on walking. When we were paying for lunch, Abby noticed that her wallet was missing from her purse. It was then that we realized that the man who had run into her had stolen her wallet. We saw a police officer on the corner and told him what happened. He told us that he was assigned to traffic duty and that we should go to a station to report it. Of course we were running late, so that had to wait until later. Nothing was going to keep Abby from seeing the latest Broadway show.

After we left the show, Abby noticed a police station. Perfect—she could report her wallet stolen there. But

they told her that she would have to report her robbery
to the precinct where the crime occurred. Strike two for
the New York City police!

Well, there was no time to find the right police
station at that point. We had tickets to an evening show,
and available cabs are hard to find at that time on a
Saturday night. Finally, after the show and dinner, we
made our way back to the North Precinct. By that time
it was after midnight and Abby was running out of
patience. They should make this whole victim-of-a-crime
thing a lot easier!

Things didn't get any better when she was told
to take a seat in the lobby and wait her turn. We soon
realized that we were the only ones there to report
a crime. Everyone else was there because they had
committed a crime. That didn't stop Abby from loudly
complaining about the cops' poor customer service and
total lack of compassion.

At last, Abby was called from behind the glass
window and asked to fill out the necessary paperwork.
As we were strolling out the door, Abby stopped, looked
at the assembled group of New York's finest, and asked,
"After the day we have had, aren't you even going to call
us a cab?" There was a moment of jaw-dropping silence
before one young officer shook his head in amazement,
grinned, and said, "Come on, ladies. Follow me." He
walked us to the corner, stopped traffic, and hailed us a
cab. I can still remember Abby's parting words: "Hey, it's

life and we're living it. Other people are just watching it on TV."

Sandy Powers's daughter Melissa became a member of the original ALDC in 1980. At the time, Sandy made the mistake of volunteering her expert services. She has been making bows, sewing costumes, creating headpieces, writing lyrics, feeding children, collecting tuition, and keeping the peace for the past thirty years.

DON'T BE A CHEAPSKATE

A child should never leave to go anywhere without money. I don't care if your kids are five years old. Put five bucks in their backpack, in their little purse, in their pocket, in their shoe, or inside their sock.

Things have changed a lot (and if you've seen *Dance Moms,* you'd agree not necessarily for the better). I used to take kids to competitions by themselves without parents. The kids were all supposed to have an envelope of money for each day. The parents, kids, and I would go through the information before leaving home for the competition and I would break down the expenses by the day: This is day one, and we're going to travel to this city and incur these expenses. We're going to be in the airport, then take a taxi, then check into the hotel, and we have to get into our room with all our luggage. This means they need ones and fives for tipping. (Your delicate daughter is seventy pounds soaking wet. Her luggage weighs in at two hundred pounds. Who is going to carry it? Not me!) On such and such a day we are going out to dinner someplace nice. Or we're going to Disney World and they're going to need more money because they must purchase a hopper pass to get into the park, they'll need food, and they may want to buy a souvenir. The next day all they need is lunch money because they'll be going to class all day, and then there's a banquet at night that is already paid for along with the competition fees.

I would go over each day's itinerary and break it down by activities and their costs. That way, a sealed envelope with the correct amount of money to cover all the estimated expenses for that day would accompany each dancer. In addition, I wanted every kid to have a hundred dollars in an emergency envelope, just in case those Katy Perry tickets come through. Remember— I've been taking kids on the road to attend competitions for more than twenty-five years. Many of my guidelines predate the debit cards and ATMs that make getting cash a lot easier today.

In those early days, before I learned better, I would end up giving twenty dollars to the valet who took the luggage out of the car and another twenty when the bellman came up to the room. I would always hear "Oh, I'm going to pay you back" or "Oh, we'll pay the next time." Then the next time comes and the kids are in class or at an audition, so I'm checking out of the hotel and I'm stuck paying again. So I've learned after all these years to collect money from the kids in advance, and then when I have to pay for something, I use their money, not mine. I hate asking the kids for money, but why am I paying for those kids when their dads are doctors and engineers and their moms are corporate vice presidents and lawyers? It's bad enough I'm babysitting them for a whole week. What would it cost them to hire a nanny to do my job?

Eventually, I started giving the kids the job of paying for everything. I would say, "Sarah, you're in charge of the tipping when we get to the hotel," or "Amanda, you're going to pay the taxi driver." This way they take on the responsibility of collecting the money from everybody so that I don't look like I'm taking money from poor inno-cent children. Plus they learn the value of a dollar, and don't think that somebody else is always going to take care of paying for them all their lives.

Then there are those times when you have a kid who leaves her envelope in the dance bag and the dance bag is locked in the car. The car is in the parking garage and we're at a restaurant hundreds of yards away. I had this one kid who never seemed to have any money with her when she needed it, and expected everyone else to pay her way. She danced with two beautiful girls—Koree and Allie, who lived in her neighborhood. They were tall and blond, and she was secretly envious of them because she was this little pip-squeak who was very talented, but a little too big for her britches. She was tiny, like four feet two or something, and they were five feet seven or eight. Their moms and dads were all friends socially.

One day when we were in New York City at some barbecue place, they got sick and tired of her because she didn't have her money again. These two fourteen-year-olds, Koree and Allie, looked at me and said, "Let her starve." They just wanted her to sit there and watch us all eat, because they were finished with her excuses and tired of their teammate always trying to scam a free meal.

There's one in every crowd, and she learns from the best: her parents. She never has her money with her! She always has to bum money to buy a snack, to eat dinner after the competition, or to purchase a T-shirt. It gets real old real fast. She tries to hide it from me, and then when that kid goes to the bathroom, her friends can't wait to tell me, "Brittany just asked us for money again."

Money is something most parents just don't teach their children about in general. Tipping, for example. Kids need to know the basics: for example, tip on the cost of the meal, not on cost plus tax; tip differently for a buffet than in a four-star restaurant. Most young people do not even realize that they have to tip. They look at the price of what they ordered—eighteen dollars for chicken Parmesan, a Coke for two-fifty—and hand me a twenty. "Isn't that close enough?" they ask. There are ways to teach children these social skills before they embarrass themselves—and you!

Every once in a while parents will give their daughter money to take me out to dinner after a competition. And she'll say, "Miss Abby, my parents gave me this money. Can I treat you to dinner?" And I say, "You don't have to do that." And she says, "Okay," and spends that money on souvenirs. This is just negligent parenting. Know when to insist. Go to the maître d' and arrange to pick up the check. Remember, if you raise your kids to be cheap, they will put you in the least expensive old folks' home when the time comes (and it just might be coming sooner than you think!).

And don't take what doesn't belong to you. Like when one of the girls orders room service and it comes to the room while she's still in the shower. By the time she gets out of the shower, somebody else in the room has eaten half the food. She didn't pay for it, but she ate it. Or if we're in a mall and there's a candy store, each one of the girls goes in and buys candy. When we get back to the room that night, the girls leave their candy on the dresser and somebody else comes along and eats some. Then they end up having this big huge argument over candy. Didn't you learn in kindergarten that if it's not yours, don't touch it? If parents would send enough money with their kids, then everyone would have money for candy and not be tempted to sample someone else's.

If you borrow something, put it back where it belongs. Don't ask somebody if you can use her hair spray or her eyelash glue and then empty the can or leave the lid off the eyelash glue so it dries out. This just makes you look like a "user," and you should be thoughtful of others' things. This kind of behavior demonstrates that you are selfish, and I have found that selfish plus sneaky equals cheap. Don't be a cheapskate! Dance studios, dance competitions, and dancers are a microcosm of life, and I'm raising my students to be successful in dance as well as in life.

. . . .

Dear Abby:

My daughter seems to get injured constantly in dance class. She falls and splits her lip. She pulls a muscle. She twists her knee. Is there any way to prevent at least some of these injuries?

When you look at a dance studio and inquire about lessons, you should also check out what substance their floors are made of. Perhaps your daughter is dancing on a surface not conducive to the art of dance. On the other hand, maybe your daughter just can't keep up with the rest of the class. When one of these so-called injuries occurs, she gets to sit out on the sidelines and avoid the risk of embarrassment that comes with going across the floor one at a time and possibly being made fun of by the other kids because she can't keep up. I would try to investigate and get to the bottom of all these injuries. It could be they are legit and your kid's a klutz.

Abby

. . . .

MEAN GIRL BEHAVIOR

Mean girl behavior begins when girls say mean things behind each other's backs. A mean girl is somebody who plays people off against each other. A mean girl is somebody who's sweet, nice, and polite in front of adults, in front of teachers, faculty, or coaches, but behind closed doors, she will throw you on the ground and step all over you. She will take your costume and hide it. She will take a brand-new soda that you just opened and spill it. She will take a bite of the doughnut that you have been saving on a napkin for after dance class and then throw it away. That's a mean girl.

We have a lot of trouble with girls who forget their props and then take someone else's. Like, for example, when I have each girl bring a chair as a prop for a routine. Sometimes when it comes to bigger items like this, I make each girl responsible for bringing one from the studio. I would have to rent a truck to get all the props to the competition if I didn't have each dancer bring her own. When someone forgets to bring her chair or leaves her chair in Dad's car and he's two hundred miles away at a business conference, a mean girl will just grab someone else's chair, and when the owner of that chair goes back to get it, she can't find it. Mean girls are sneaky and they are liars, and rather than coming to me and saying, "I forgot my chair—what are we going to do?" they steal somebody else's and pretend it's theirs. Then if their mother can go get a chair and get it back to the competition in time, two minutes before they go out onstage, another chair magically appears.

I have seen the same thing happen with dance shoes. The mean girl has her shoes in the studio and takes them off to run through the routine. When she is finished dancing for the day, she walks out of the studio—accidentally leaving her dance shoes behind. The next day at a competition three hours away from the studio on a Saturday night, the mean girl realizes she doesn't have her dance shoes. Guess what? She puts on somebody else's jazz shoes who wears the same size, because she knows it's hard to tell whose shoes they are once they are on your feet. How would anyone know they weren't your shoes? A lot of sneaky, dishonest stuff like that happens among girls. It's not always that the mean girl is trying to sabotage those who have their acts together. It's just that she's trying to save her own ass. This poor behavior stems from forgetfulness, immaturity, a lack of trust, and of course poor parenting skills.

ABBY'S ULTIMATE ADVICE
Three Key Points to Remember

1. Remember: when there's a crown on your head, somebody's watching.

2. Don't interrupt the instructor when she's teaching— this goes for students and for moms alike!

3. Teach your children the value of money and the importance of paying their own way. Make sure they always have money in their pockets.

SIXTH POSITION
EFFACÉ

Second Place Is the First One to Lose

> The most effective way to do it is to do it.
> —*Amelia Earhart*

BY "SECOND PLACE IS THE FIRST ONE TO LOSE," I mean you are the biggest loser on that stage. You are the defeated man on the track. You are the horse, but you're not in the winner's circle. If a thousand people show up, somebody wins and somebody's in second place. If you take nine hundred and ninety-eight people away from that and two people show up, somebody wins and somebody loses.

Sometimes it is better to be third than to be second, and often they'll use the term *first runner-up*. You have the winner and you have the first runner-up. That is the worst place to be, because you came so close, but you lost and you didn't get the glory. You put the work in and did everything right, but you got beat. If you get third place, you're like "Woo-hoo, I placed! I got something." In the Olympics, you're still out there on the podium. You still have a medal around your neck.

The irony is that the first runner-up is the person who makes it into the Broadway show six months later, on television dancing in *Smash,* or dancing backup for Kanye West. In the case of dance competitions, odds are you'll never hear from the winner again. Could this entire endeavor have been orchestrated for them? It was all about just winning first place, and it was orchestrated for them, and they're never going to be anything else.

There's a nonprofit organization, which shall remain nameless but certainly not faceless, that I used to belong to and it's run by volunteers. Newsflash: if people are willing to volunteer their time and energy, there's something in it for them. When somebody volunteers to run the competition for this organization, they take on a great responsibility. This position is all-consuming. They must secure a theater, convince others to help run the show, and among many other responsibilities find five suitable judges who don't know any of the contestants or teachers involved. Good luck with that! In all my years of attending, the judges know everybody. More than likely this organizer will ask five of her friends to judge.

For example, one judge has a student in one age division of the competition, so the person who's running that section of the competition has her judge a different division from her own student's of course. But then a buddy of hers ends up judging that student's age division, and she wins. It's kind of like "You scratch my back, I'll scratch yours." The whole organization is very incestuous. Now,

I've had my fair share of prestigious winners. Just to set the record straight, I have been the proud teacher of Petite Miss Dance of America, Junior Miss Dance of America, Teen Miss Dance of America, Teen Mister Dance of America, Miss Dance of America, and Mister Dance of America. These victories have not come easily. These dancers were the lucky ones who overcame all those hoping they wouldn't win. I've had so many kids screwed over who should have won but didn't. Their scores are so high and they're so talented that the judges can't have them place fourth or fifth because that would be too obvious. So they place these kids high, but they're careful with tenths of a point to make sure that kid doesn't win first place but instead wins first runner-up. I have lots of first runners-up who have gone on to surpass the titleholders and have lucrative careers as successful, employable dancers. They're like dandelions; you can't keep them down.

The directors in charge would never cheat mathematically, but among other things they do create the lineups, which is the order in which dancers perform their routines for the competition. For example, if there are thirty girls competing, they would put their friend's girl last to give her the leg up on the competition. By controlling the lineup, you can control when this dancer performs and who she follows. Your number also comes into play during audition classes. Where you stand and who you're with plays an important part of any title competition. For example, to give a contestant an advantage, you could put her in numerical order right after somebody who you know is pretty weak. All of these things come into play during a competition.

Sure, there's no *I* in *team,* but there is an *M* and an *E.* And sometimes it's all about *me.* I want my top students to represent the Abby Lee Dance Company onstage whenever possible. Winning is important because it lets you know you're on the right track and it bestows confidence. But there's a lot that goes into winning that doesn't happen on the stage. Most of all, it's the work that went into the win. The will that went into the win.

I preach to my students over and over. When it comes time for kids to enter the big competitions, or what we refer to as "titles," some bow out gracefully. They are the real losers. I don't know whether they are lazy or scared to death. They say they don't need all the hoopla to prove themselves as great dancers. When it's all over, it's not the crown, the banner, and the trophy that make you a champion but the hours of training you put in preparing for the win. When we look back, the crown has lost a few stones, the banner is frayed, and the trophy is tarnished, but your dedication will continue to pay off forever.

There are a lot of little secrets to winning that are not exactly secrets. Common sense is not a secret, but if I could put it in a bottle and sell it, I'd be a very rich woman. For starters, your child will learn by example; it's important to study other dancers. We went to one competition that was in a gymnasium, and our star dancer wore her jazz shoes out onto that slick wood floor. She tried to do an aerial front walkover but got nervous midair and changed her mind to execute a diving front walkover instead. When she planted her foot, it slid right out from under her and she fell on her hip. Our next dancer took her shoes off and went barefoot. It's not what she planned, but she learned from another's mistake. And once your kid wins, everyone will be watching for *her* to make a mistake. As I tell my students, *it's hard to get to the top of the pyramid, but it's even tougher to stay there.*

On the flip side, if you see your child struggling—and I don't mean working hard, I mean *struggling*—it may be time to ask yourself if she or he is in the right place. Are you pushing her into something she doesn't really want or is unable to do? Is he really an AP student, talented dancer, or star athlete?

. . . .

Dear Abby:
My daughter is fourteen and wants to begin dance lessons.
Besides very little to no dance experience, she isn't flexible at all.
What can she do to increase her flexibility? Or is it too late?

It is never too late to dance. Your fourteen-year-old daughter may be interested in auditioning for her high school musical or the school play, something that involves movement, so I think it would be great for her to take a jazz class or a ballet class or perhaps both. As far as flexibility goes, that's free and you can certainly work on it at home. Get your butt down into that split, and if you can't do it, blame yourself, because if you want to be in a split you'll get in a split. It takes time and repetition, but you can do it.

. . . .

BE TRUTHFUL WITH YOURSELF

When I say, "Be truthful with yourself," I think about kids looking in the mirror and seeing something else. They think they're good and that they're working hard. They think they're on the right foot when they're not. Again, times have changed. Years ago, the girls in my senior company looked in the mirror and somebody knew when she was off and corrected herself. One kid would open her mouth to another person and ask her why she was late on the counts. They would bicker between each other about who was right and who was wrong. They used to look in the mirror and make the necessary corrections and help each other.

I think one out of one hundred children is born with natural rhythm. Another nine can learn it. The other ninety, oh well.

The kids used to step up and say, "I'm late. We just did the dance ten times and I was late ten times. What am I doing wrong? Can somebody go over it with me?"

Kids today don't do that. They just do it wrong time after time after time because they think they look good. Why wouldn't they? Their moms are telling them how great they are every five seconds.

But if they aren't in front of a mirror, sometimes I'll ask, "Do you wear contacts?" If they say, "No, why?" I'll say, "Because you're seeing through rose-colored glass, and I don't know where you found that rose-colored glass because it's not in this room. Here there is only clear glass." I want my dancers to open their eyes and see what's really going on—be truthful with yourself! When I look in the mirror, I see a size six Prada. Unfortunately, nobody else does.

Natural ability has to be taken into account. The genes handed down from generation to generation count. Was your child born with the facility and body type for the future she desires? If this isn't your child, evaluate her other talents. Some of my kids are great dancers and average students in school; they want to be stars for a living. I ask them, "Do you want to go to college or do you want to dance?" You have to assess your options. Is the choice between a scholarship to Harvard and dancing on a cruise ship? It's a no-brainer—go to Harvard! Or is the choice between heading up Route 79 to a Pennsylvania state school with a boatload of student loans or starring on Broadway at the age of eighteen? Big difference.

. . . .

Dear Abby:

My daughter just won a competition, and I would like to give her dance teacher a gift to show our thanks. What do you suggest?

I can tell you what you shouldn't get your kid's dance instructor—don't buy a big flower arrangement and have it delivered to the dance studio. That says, "Look at me—I just won a competition!" It's not personal—it's something that everyone is going to see at the studio, and in a few days it's going to end up in the trash can. If your kid's instructor has gone above and beyond, then by all means get her a gift, but make it something that's both personal and useful. I suggest a department store or gas gift card, or if she's a coffee lover, then a Starbucks gift card. I guarantee you that these gestures of thanks won't go unnoticed by your kid's instructor, and it just might make a difference when she is making a decision about who to give a solo to or who to feature in a group performance.

Abby

. . . .

FAILURE MAKES YOU STRONGER

If you have the ability to pick yourself up by the boot-straps and start over, you come out stronger because you learn from whatever mistakes you made. This goes for me too. I've made a lot of mistakes in my past. I'm thinking now of the time I put all my eggs in one basket by putting too much love, heart, soul, time, and energy into one kid. That kid I was doing it for ended up stabbing me in the back.

At the age of fourteen, when I set out to produce amazing, talented, employable dancers, never once did I think about making a million dollars. I'm living in my parents' house right now because I moved back home when my dad was sick. There are probably ten boxes of costumes in our garage that people never paid for from twenty to forty years ago. I feel like my business practices at the front desk are not as tough as my lessons inside the dance studio. I let people take advantage of me for years. All those kids whom I took away to competitions year after year. I bought them meals and I paid for them when they left their money in the car, and a few of these same kids don't even send a Christmas card. I want these kids and their parents to remember where they came from, and that if it weren't for me, they wouldn't be where they are today.

Some moms criticize me and say I put too much pressure on the kids to win. I set the bar high because I know what these kids are capable of. I know when they're giving it their all and I know when they're being lazy. So yes, I turn the heat up. I tell them I will not accept losing to the Crabby Apples or any other team out there. Why? Because we're better than they are. Dance teachers have to be tough and they have to push hard. If you don't, you wind up with a team full of slugs. I believe *everyone* needs motivation.

Something I have heard at several business seminars is "Don't worry about what the ballet teacher is getting paid, worry about what the woman at the front desk is getting paid." I never had to worry, because my dad ran my business. He was the one at the front desk. He was the one who had to chase the kid all the way out to the parking lot to get the parents to come in and pay. Daddy always had my back. My dad had impeccable credit, and Mom and I never had to worry about money. Not until he was diagnosed with a brain tumor. We had no idea that he was going to the studio, day in and day out. However, the work was still piling up. Suddenly, I found myself in charge of everything business related. Finances were fine by me—I had no problem spending money.

When something doesn't work, I get angry at myself. I take time to think it through and figure out why it didn't work, and what I have learned from my mistake. Children have to go through the same thought process. Every kid needs to lose once in a while, even your best. They are always hearing that they are stars and that they are the most amazing kids. If they just keep winning, that victory becomes worthless because it's expected. So you want to keep them a little bit vulnerable. You want to keep them on their toes. Dancers always have to strive for perfection, but they never reach it.

I think failure is good in one sense, whether it's in

business, art, or sports, because then when you do discover greatness, when you do have that glorious victory,
then it's a taste of euphoria.

Pro sports athletes make millions of dollars. They
should not go out on the field and fail. They should not have
to pick themselves up by their bootstraps. They should go
out and the score should be 0–0, or the score should be
21–21 because both teams are that good. Someone who
is making millions of dollars shouldn't fumble the ball. I
think that these players should get paid at the end of the
season once we see how well they play.

The kid who never fails is never the big winner. You
need to be knocked down a few notches every now and
then so you can keep your eye on the big prize.

. . . .

Dear Abby:
My daughter seems to be struggling with remembering her
choreography. Do you have any tips to help her remember?

Some kids pick up choreography quickly and some kids don't.
I have found that attending dance conventions, workshops,
and seminars helps children pick up choreography quicker.
You're learning from a different teacher every hour and
you're learning a new style from that teacher. So these
events teach you to better comprehend choreography. Eight
hundred kids can go into the convention class. Four hundred
will learn the routine perfectly and be able to perform it at

the end of the class. The other four hundred will have no clue what the combination was or what the steps were. We all make choices. Have you taught your child how to make the right choice?

Abby

. . . .

FEAR SHOULD NEVER STAND IN YOUR WAY

Don't be afraid that somebody is going to say something about you or that somebody is not going to like something you do. With the *Dance Moms* TV show, I had no idea what I was getting into. It was uncharted waters, but I didn't let fear stand in my way. I didn't know that much about television. The only thing I *did* know was that I had watched it my whole life. I was an only child and the TV was my very best friend. I loved television. I love scripted TV. I could probably recite every word from every *Brady Bunch* episode ever made. Years ago, when I was around thirteen or fourteen, I used to watch this television show called *Blossom*. At the beginning of the show, Blossom would be tap-dancing on top of a piano. I used to sit there watching this show and think to myself, "If she can have a television show, anybody can!"

I'm sure people look at me on their television sets and think the exact same thing!

When I took a shot at having my own TV show, it all happened so fast that the next thing I knew I was sign-

ing on the dotted line for fifteen hundred dollars an episode for four years with an option for eight. And while
that may seem like a lot of money to some, you have to
remember that I film six days a week, twelve or more
hours a day. In addition, my studio has become a set. So
the income I had always gained from teaching classes is
no longer coming in.

When the show first started airing, I didn't have
much visibility yet among the general public outside of
dance circles, but many of my dance colleagues and com-
petitors across the country saw the show and were out-
raged. There were many more naysayers than fans. I have
learned that people who have something negative to say
are heard loud and clear—they write letters, they send
e-mails, they make phone calls to voice their complaints.
People who have good things to say, however, don't take
the time to write or call. After the very first episode aired,
the members of the dance teaching industry lost their
minds. They all know me, they know my standards of
excellence, they know my teaching methods, they know
how I run my school, and they are well aware of my credentials and what I have produced in the way of winning
students and working professionals. However, this was
their big chance to slam Abby Lee Miller.

And that they did.

Articles were written, blogs created, and hate mail
was sent—all from my bitter and most competitive colleagues. In reality, they just couldn't stand the fact that

they didn't think of *Dance Moms* first, or that they and their studios weren't chosen by the producers. It didn't help that when Lifetime aired the promos for the very first episodes they were showing me with a baseball bat in my hand (it was a foam rubber toy). Flash to one of the beautiful girls crying over and over. In the meantime, this child was in pain because her mother burned her with a curling iron, which had absolutely nothing to do with me. The editors can manipulate footage to create something out of nothing. The whole thing was preposterous.

On day one, Collins Avenue Entertainment, the production company that sold our show, along with Lifetime, the network that bought our show, started the uproar by depicting me as the tough but talented teacher. This negative light has continued to generate controversy throughout the four consecutive seasons. When it comes to reality TV, I guess I'm doing something right. Then I gradually morphed into being recognized in public, with people stalking me and talking to me. Once you stop shooting an episode, all the camera crews and the hype go away and you're back to your regular grunt work. Yet now the show is airing on TV, so I would be at the grocery store or having dinner at a restaurant, and people are staring at me. I'm thinking I must know these people because their kid used to take dancing. Let's face it, I've had thousands of kids pass through my studio.

Now that we're in Season Four, I can't go anywhere without being recognized. Usually it's wonderful. No matter how hateful they make me look on TV, people always want to hug me. Children run toward me and jump into my arms at the grocery store. I guess they can sense my big heart and that I love children. I don't always feel like hugging everyone, but I do. My only complaint is when I don't have my hair and makeup done and I'm wearing a pair of sweats. People want a picture, so then I give them a picture and then they put it all over social media and I look like crap. But I am always kind and gracious because without fans we wouldn't have a show.

At the beginning, I didn't know anything about making a TV show, but I thought if I didn't go for this, somebody else would. Once again, everyone's replaceable. So I'm going to make this reality TV show happen. I figured at least I would learn something about making television. I view fear as a handicap and think your own phobias hold you back. I've never been afraid of what other people are going to say, what other people are going to think, or what other people are going to do in response to my actions.

Even if you're afraid, you have to do what you feel is best for yourself. If you're afraid of everything, then you're going to curl up in a ball and die. It's a big, scary, mean place out there in the world. Everyone has anxiety and insecurity. Encourage your children not to cower but to face their fears head on. You can't be afraid to walk down the street to get to that concert, to get to class on time, or to visit that store. You can't be afraid to get behind the wheel of a rental car in L.A. and drive up the Pacific Coast Highway. I was an adventurous seventeen years of age before they changed the laws to where now you have to be twenty-five to rent a car. I was in Anaheim, California, with my mom at a dance convention. I rented a car and drove into L.A. and saw it all. I remember this convention well because John Travolta showed up at the grand national banquet with Marilu Henner on his arm. (Little known fact: her mother owned and operated a successful dance studio.) He received an award for contributing to the art of dance. He came to accept it himself, gave a speech, and appeared very grateful. Oh, my God, he was my matinee idol. I saw *Grease* seventeen times the weekend it opened. Not only was he the heartthrob we all loved but he inspired the whole world to dance. When we saw him on-screen doing the Hustle in *Saturday Night Fever,* every middle-class couple in America signed up for disco lessons at their local dance studio. Adult jazz classes were formed for the sudden increase in students because of to his performance as a Broadway dancer in *Staying Alive.* Next came a new dance craze. When he starred in *Urban Cowboy,* every dance studio in the nation began offering country-western line dancing.

. . . .

Dear Abby:

How do you audition dancers for your competition team?

I hold an audition every August for students who want to become a part of the Abby Lee Dance Company. The first things I ask them to do are a right split, a left split, and a straddle split. Then I make a cut. I want to see who is flexible and what their body alignment looks like right off the bat. Then I do ballet steps to see if they know their terminology, and tap to check their rhythm and timing, and to see if they can actually count out the tap steps. Then acrobatics, a simple standing backbend. I can tell a great deal about their flexibility and potential from a basic standing backbend. I move quickly to a chin stand, full back split, hand walks, back handsprings, aerial cartwheels, and aerial walkovers. I am always looking for dancers accomplished in all genres, as well as smart dancers who are quick and creative. Then we teach a short combination to see if they can pick it up right away. The innate ability to comprehend movement quickly is the essential gift every great dancer is born with. And looks are important too. Let the hopefuls show off and see what they can do. This is called improv. I want to see what a dancer brings to the audition. And as long as their parents' credit checks out, then we're good to go. This may sound harsh but I am running a business. I have learned from my mistakes, much more slowly than my students do, I'm afraid to say. Letting all the Chloes continue to take class when their parents couldn't afford the luxury is not how I do business anymore. When you don't pay, it's called an after-school activity. When you do pay, it's respecting one's vocation. Nice guys finish last. Letting all those innocent ingenues I cared so much about go without paying for months at a time put my building and my livelihood in jeopardy.

Abby

· ·

DON'T BE MEDIOCRE

One of my less-than-brilliant moms always used to say, "I just want my kids to be happy. I don't care if they're mediocre." Who the hell wants mediocre kids? Why don't you want your kids to be the best that they can be? Maybe it's not dance. Maybe it's not music or the recording industry. Maybe it's being a nurse or a doctor, but why don't you want them to be the best nurse or doctor they can be? Why do anything half-assed? If you're not going to do it 100 percent, then don't do it.

I don't subscribe to mediocre. I think that there are kids who love to dance and they do it for fun, to learn, to get off the couch and get some exercise. Or they dance because they like to be onstage. They like the theatrics of musicals and the television show *Glee*. That's all fine, but I'm talking about members of the elite Abby Lee Dance Company competition team. These wannabes want it all. They want to be amazing. They want to be the best. They want to be on Broadway. They want to be inside the industry in any way they can. Half of the TV crew that works on our show is filled with people who moved to Hollywood to find fame and fortune in the entertainment industry as an actor or actress, or as a writer or director—and they failed. Now they call themselves producers, and they're not too good at that either. Then there are the kids who love to dance and work really hard, but don't have the talent. They just don't have what it takes, but they work like dogs. They want it. They breathe, sleep, and eat it.

Then there are the kids who are lazy. I think they would rather lie in their beds and talk on their phones than work hard at anything. When traveling for competitions, I have seen Brooke's mom, Kelly, apply all Brooke's makeup and put her eyelashes on—all while Brooke was snuggled in her bed! Kelly would wake up before dawn and ever so gently transform Brooke's face into performance perfection. When the princess finally woke up and got out of bed to brush her teeth, she would startle herself in the mirror. Mirror, mirror on the wall, who's the fairest of them all?

If you're going to choose to be mediocre, I think it's better to quit than to pull others down with you. On the flip side of that, I once had a girl who was Miss Dance of America who just up and quit one day. You are on top of the world, top of the pyramid, top of the heap, and you give it all up? That is the epitome of laziness. Earlier in this book I said getting to the top is hard but staying there is even tougher. Well, this young adult obviously wasn't up for the challenge. Rumors were ablaze: she had to go to a special summer program to get into college. She had to do *something* because dance wasn't in her future anymore. Nobody really knows the truth. It was all very strange. More important, it was a huge waste of all the time, energy, and expertise that I had put into her.

I have a boy this year who is amazing. He's been with me since he was eight years old. He has had several scenes on my TV show. He's a beautiful dancer, but he's lazy. I caught him skipping all these classes at the national convention and doing all sorts of things he shouldn't have been doing. He's not behaviorally bad, he's just a bit lazy. He doesn't consistently come to the studio. He missed a lot of time in the studio and then came back one day in September and took a class. He was fine and could still do everything. He disappeared again and came back one day at the beginning of October and had lost some of his flexibility. He wasn't as on top of his game and as great a dancer as he was during the summer. I'm waiting to see if he shows up in November. I'm starting to feel he's a once-a-month student. It's a weird situation with the mom and dad and they're having a lot of troubles at home. I offered him a partial tuition fellowship, and I helped him out financially so that he could go to Nationals. I brought him on the TV show and that provided him with yet another wonderful opportunity. After doing all of these things for him, I realized that this kid doesn't even walk into the room and say hello to me. So I said, "No. Forget it. You don't want it? Quit then!"

HOW TO INTERVIEW

Someday you may find yourself interviewing for a dance job. Sometimes it comes down to not just how you dance, but who you are. After all, if you're going to be working side by side with someone onstage or on a tour day after day, you want to know that it's someone you *like!* There's a right and a wrong way to respond to the questions you'll be asked. Here are some sample questions and answers, all of which are meant to convey confidence, intelligence, verve, and even wit:

What do you think about Obama winning the election?
   My parents taught me never to discuss religion or politics.

If you could be a flower, what flower would you be and why?
   I would be a dandelion because you can't keep me down.

What three things would you bring to a desert island?
   The Professor, Ginger, and Mary Ann.

Rate yourself on a scale of one to ten.
   I'm a nine because there's always room for improvement.

How old are you?
   How old do you need me to be?

The high schooler who gets the best SAT score doesn't always win the scholarship. The most qualified applicant doesn't always get the job. It's just a truth of life that presentation is everything. For example, my students start interviewing at the age of eight, and I teach them exactly how to do it, the same way they learn their routines. The most important part is making a good first impression. This includes everything from what they wear (*Buy the two-hundred-dollar shoes even if you have to return them the next day!*) to how they walk (*Enter the room boobs first! Chest out; stand tall!*). I even tell my kids how to sit: *You don't walk over to the chair, look at it, and sit down. Feel the chair with the backs of your legs.* You have to believe in what you're selling: *you.*

ABBY'S ULTIMATE ADVICE
Three Key Points to Remember

1. Be honest with yourself about your strengths and weaknesses. Recognize and admit to your faults and commit to correcting them.

2. Don't let fear get in between you and your dreams. Face your fears head-on!

3. Be amazing, be remarkable, be happy—be *anything* but mediocre!

SEVENTH POSITION
À LA QUATRIÈME DERRIÈRE

Contracts Aren't Meant to Be Broken

> The only place where success comes
> before work is in the dictionary.
> —*Vince Lombardi*

I HAVE NO TOLERANCE FOR QUITTERS. They waste my time and everyone else's time too. As I mentioned earlier, kids quit my dance classes for two reasons: they can't cut it or they can't afford to pay. Contrary to popular belief or town gossip, my studio is not expensive! Some moms are serial studio-hoppers; they like to sample this and that, and wind up driving their kids nuts and discouraging them in the process.

A child who is a serious competitor at any age in any field will have to become more independent. At the Jacqueline Kennedy Onassis School at the American Ballet Theatre, dancers are pretty much living on their own in New York City at the age of eleven. Joshua Waitzkin became an International Master of chess at the age of sixteen. Serena Williams won the U.S. Open when she was seventeen, after touring the world competitively for years. To be the best at what they do, competitive youngsters have to move around, and this requires them to be autonomous. My students travel most weekends, whether it's just from their homes to the studio or to competitions all over the country.

One time a mom called me to say her daughter couldn't make it to practice because there was no one to drive her. I told this mom to send her teenager in a taxi, and she freaked out—had a conniption. I'm talking about a fourteen-year-old young woman here, and her mother is afraid to let her get in a car with a driver who is bonded and insured so she can get to class on time. The mom would have preferred that her kid go with a sixteen-year-old boy from the neighborhood who had just gotten his license last week. Does this make any sense? Who lost out? Her daughter sat on her butt all evening while everyone else had four hours of training to become better, stronger, and smarter.

If you sign a contract to do something, there's a duration during which you must honor it. If you signed a contract for six months, then you have to commit for six months. If it's for a year, then you're in deep for a year. When parents let their kids quit before they have fulfilled their commitment, those kids are going to end up attending five different colleges before they finally receive a degree. When they take a tough class they're going to say, "Oh, geez, this class is a hard one; I think I better just drop it." And they will. Remember, you taught them this is okay.

When your daughter brings home her very first club flyer from school and wants to join the Brownies, it's about making a commitment. She would make a commitment to stay after school from 4:00 P.M. to 5:00 P.M. once a week. She would make a commitment to make crafts, earn badges, go camping, and sell Girl Scout cookies.

In my house and in my neighborhood, we didn't go around and sell things. When I was a Girl Scout, my mom wrote a check and bought all the cookies, and then gave them to people. A high school girl up the street from me had a dad who was president of a big company in Pittsburgh. One day when she came to our house selling candy for the high school marching band to go on a class trip to Walt Disney World to perform in the parade, without missing a beat, my dad told her to have her old man write a check for her vacation to Orlando—he could certainly afford it.

Now I know that kids have to sell things to raise money. It's the American way. You name it, the Abby Lee Dance Company sold it! I'll bet you that my original members from 1980 to 1995 could recite to you "Three ham, three salami, two cappicola, two provolone, lettuce, onions, and tomato in a separate baggie in the hoagies." We actually made all the sandwiches ourselves and then the kids went out and delivered them. I'm embarrassed to admit that I miss the smell of those oven-fresh Italian rolls.

When you commit your child to an activity, as a parent, you need to be responsible for your child seeing it through. This is the parent's responsibility as much as it is the child's, so explain the commitment to your child.

Go over it. If you don't want to sign up again next year, that's fine, but come hell or high water, you're going to be in that recital this year and do whatever it takes to get there. When all your friends are outside playing in May and June, and you have to come inside and put on a leotard and tights to get to your dance class, you're doing it because you made a commitment. You have a place in the group, and people are counting on you.

We do not live in a selfish world. We live in a world where you must think of others. For so many people, it's all about them. Forget about everybody else! What if you're in a group routine that has partners and there are twelve kids? Suddenly you quit and there are only eleven kids. What does the kid without a partner do now?

I believe that you have to give kids the wings to fly. Start off small, make sure that you can trust them (and if you've done a good job parenting, you can), then cut them a little slack. Or even better, cut them a *lot* of slack.

. . . .

Dear Abby:
I've owned a dance studio for two years. I'm thinking about starting a competition team. What do you think attending competitions does for your studio?

Some studio owners have great recreation programs, with kids who come and have fun. Then they start a competition team and end up losing money and losing students because the kids don't want all the extra rehearsals, the time commitment, the pressure to be better—they just want the sweatshirt, the jacket, and the glory. So the answer is, I think competition can be a great thing. It's going to motivate your dancers to improve. It could help your business because students will want private lessons. They'll want to come to extra classes and pay for rehearsals so they have the edge up at a competition. However, it could also be detrimental. You don't want your students to see the studio down the street winning everything at a competition, because then they'll end up there.

Abby

. . . .

DON'T PUNISH YOUR KIDS BY TAKING AWAY THINGS THAT ARE GOOD FOR THEM

Years ago I used to have a lot of parents who would reprimand their children by taking dance classes away. If kids got bad grades on their report cards, Mom and Dad pulled them out of dance class, rushing them home to study. I always thought these parents were kind of dumb because they were paying for the kids to come to dance class yet punishing them by not letting them come to a class they'd already paid for. But not only were they punishing their kids, they were inadvertently punishing everybody else on the team too. You sign a contract that you're going to pay for ten months from September to

June, whether your kid comes or not. You can't call and say your daughter is taking the month off until she gets her grades up. The child needs to know that her grades have to stay up in order to be in these activities. That's part of the commitment.

Also, you're punishing your kids by taking away something that could be their future. They might have been destined to become a professional dancer someday, and here you're taking away that possibility through punishment. Kids love what comes easy. Not everybody is book smart. Not everybody is a scholar. It takes all types to make the world go around. You need to look at dance from all angles and realize that. I've had many parents tell me that the investment they made in dance—for tuition, costumes, traveling, and competition—could have paid for college. I'm sure that's true, but not every kid's best path is to go directly to college after he or she graduates from high school.

From ninth grade to their senior year, when your kids are dancing twenty hours a week, *that* is their future. They're already working toward their first dance job right out of high school. They've already put those years in and landed their first job on Broadway—their big break, making great money—while their friends are off at college and grad school. Dance is their first job, and it's a vocation that they must take seriously. That's why I say, "Don't punish your kids by taking away things that are good for them."

ABBY LEE DANCE COMPANY WORKING DANCERS

Allie Meixner

Ashley Kacvinsky

Asmeret Ghebremichael

Bethenny Flora

Brandon Pent

Brooke Hyland

Chloe Lukasiak

Claire Taormina

Emily Burkhart

Emily Shoop

Erin Murphy

Gianna Martello

Heather Snyder

Ira Cambric

James Washington

Jennifer Snyder

Jennine Wedge

Jesse Johnson

Jessica Ice

Jessica Sweesey

John Michael Fiumara

Katie Hackett

Kendall Vertes

Kirsten Bracken

Koree Kurkowski

Kristi Grachen

Lindsey Hensler

Lisa Shontz

Mackenzie Ziegler

Maddie Ziegler

Marissa Pampena

Mark Myars

Megan Kovitch

Michelle Pampena

Miranda Maleski

Nia Frazier

Paige Hyland

Payton Ackerman

Rachael Kreiling

Sara Kosinski

Semhar Ghebremichael

Taylor Ackerman

Theresa Moio

. . . .

Dear Abby:

I run a dance studio and have one student who never makes it to class on time and almost never comes in the appropriate dancewear no matter how many times I remind the parents. I really see potential in this young dancer and don't want to lose her as a student. Do you have any suggestions?

I know you have compassion for this child, but
unfortunately there are many children with potential.
Does she have parental support? That's the big question.
I wish I could switch moms and kids around at my studio
sometimes. In your case, I think giving her a gift of a brand-
new leotard and tights would be nice, and arranging for a
ride with another student could be helpful. But remember—
sometimes the kids you do the most for are the ones who
kick you in the ass in the end.

Abby

. . . .

A CONTRACT IS A CONTRACT

In the Abby Lee Dance Company contract, things like
dyeing your hair, piercing your face, and getting a tattoo
are *not* okay. Through my contract, I am trying to teach
my kids what is acceptable in the dance world. If you go
for an audition or a job, whether it's to be in a commer-
cial or a marketing campaign, you're hired based on your
photo. If you show up looking completely different, with a
different hair cut and a different hair color from what you
had in the photo, they won't use you. Also, if you're hired
at a certain weight so that you fit into a costume and then
you drop twenty pounds, they won't use you anymore
because you're swimming in a costume that is just too big.

It's the same with being a Rockette. If they lose or
gain more than fifteen pounds, they're put on a list to be

watched. They could be fined because they won't fit into the costume. You're talking about tens of thousands of dollars' worth of satin, sequins, and rhinestones that have to be altered if you lose or gain too much weight. Whether it's a lease or a rental agreement, you have to teach your offspring to respect contracts and follow them—unlike dance mom Christi, who is teaching her daughter a different philosophy.

If the contract says you can't perform our choreography anywhere outside the studio or at competitions and you have your daughter doing our choreography all over the place to make money, what are you teaching her? Parents who disregard contracts are training their kids to skip out on their lease in the middle of the night when they get their first apartment. That's what you're teaching them.

Selling cookies is part of your contract with the Girl Scouts. You don't turn the cookies back in and say you couldn't sell them. What if everybody did that? Like the kid who is the star player on the Pop Warner football team. While the rest of the team is selling candy bars to raise money, the star player, who is a natural athlete, doesn't sell anything. If the contract reads that you have to sell a certain number of candy bars in order to play, then you should have to sell those candy bars or get benched and not be allowed to play. If the superstar player gets to play even if he doesn't sell anything, this is teaching the young player that he can break contracts, and that's not okay in my book.

If there's a contract set forth, it must be signed and

honored by all involved. Although you don't want to be a tattletale, teach your children that if they see someone breaking a contract, it's important that they bring it to the attention of the authorities.

Parents who lie about a kid's age are putting the integrity of the coach, the teacher, or the president of the club in jeopardy, and could possibly ruin the career that professional has worked so hard for. You're really playing with fire. If a wrestler is lying about his weight class, this could ruin his coach's career. You should always take contracts seriously and teach your children at a young age that, for example, this piece of paper says you're going to pick up your toys and if you don't do that, then there will be consequences. If they don't pick up their toys, then Mommy goes to the drawer to get the paper out and says, "Look, this is what you agreed to, and you aren't holding up your end of the deal." I don't think parents want to raise young adults who are going to treat society with disrespect and try to weasel out of commitments. We don't need any more of that in the world.

. . . .

Dear Abby:

I am a teacher at a dance studio and I have one parent who is causing a lot of trouble because she feels her daughter should be moved to a higher-level class. I really feel this student would benefit from a few more months, if not another year, at the level she's at. What should I do to calm this mom down?

Parents always want their child to be in with older students or at a more advanced level. I don't know why, but they do. I suggest you take the kid out of the group where she is currently, put her in the next advanced level, bury her in the back of the number, and be as tough on her as you are on the others so the mother realizes she can't keep up. You may lose a student, but it may be worth it in the long run. Stick to your rules—always. No child is worth bending your rules for, because whether that child leaves because there's another issue, problem, or conflict, or they leave when they're eighteen on a happy note, they still leave.

Abby

. . . .

ABBY'S LIFELINE AT LIFETIME
by Tim Nolan

My first introduction to Abby was not in person but by watching a behind-the-scenes video of a promo shoot my team was filming for *Dance Moms*. I'm lucky to run the marketing department for Lifetime and I take pride in my amazing creative team, so when I watched the shoot I was astonished to see how upset Abby was and thought she was being too harsh and difficult. Well, it was the lack of authenticity of the wardrobe and choreography that upset her, and I couldn't argue that, but I still had the impression that she was difficult. That would soon change.

As I spent more time with Abby I began to appreciate her style. I love people who make me laugh, so when she asked me to fulfill one of her mother's lifelong requests, how could I say no? Her mother, who was also passionate about dance, always wanted to go to the Tonys. So I worked my connections and was able to get four tickets—one each for Abby; her mom; my fiancé, Rudy; and me.

When the big night arrived, we went to pick them up at their hotel. We were all running late, not a great start! Everyone piled into the van, but the driveway of the hotel was jammed with traffic, and there was a taxi in front of us that was taking forever to load. I quietly began to worry we wouldn't make it to the show in time, and while I stewed in my own panic, I watched Abby calmly roll down her window. Without a care in the world, she shouted to the taxi customers:

"Hey, are you guys going to the Tonys?"

They looked a bit shocked and shook their heads no.

So Abby shouts, "Well, we are and we're late, so get out of the way!"

Rudy and I fell on the floor of our van laughing hysterically.

The taxi moved out of the way, and our two-block expedition began in earnest. We navigated the maze of one-way Manhattan streets, running into several blockades around Radio City Music Hall. At each blocked street, Abby rolled down her window and yelled at the cops working the corner. At one block it was "Hey—my mother is very sick and can't walk. We need to use this street." At another block, "It is imperative that I get to the Tonys—open this block!"

Now, NYC cops aren't known for being courteous, so the fact that they smiled at her and let us pass was a shock to this New Yorker.

We pulled up front, stormed the doors, and ushered Abby's mom to her seat—all in a flutter of autographs and photo ops. No sooner had we settled in, with me amazed we had made it at all, than Abby said, "Let's go get a drink," and back out to the lobby we went. I could barely keep up! More photos, more fans—"We love you!" "Can I have a pic?" "Abby, over here!"

I spent one night with Abby but I learned the lesson of a lifetime. I learned to embrace passion, have fun in life, and if people aren't going where you want to go, tell them to get out of the way and move on. You will have a good time!

Tim Nolan was named senior vice president of Marketing Creative and Brand Strategy for Lifetime Networks in 2010. Based in New York, he is responsible for overseeing all on-air, print, online, and out-of-home marketing efforts for Lifetime's scripted and reality series and original movies, as well as Lifetime Movie Network (LMN) and Lifetime Real Women.

TEACH YOUR KIDS TO KEEP COMMITMENTS

It is so important for parents to teach their kids to keep their commitments. Things like being on time and having everything they need—their equipment, uniforms, leotards, costumes, ice skates, or whatever. I feel like it's the child's responsibility first and then the parents' to follow up and make sure the kids are doing what they're supposed to be doing.

When a student isn't following through with her commitment to the dance studio, I first try to find out what's going on. Is there something wrong at home? Is there trouble in paradise? Find out what the situation is. If it turns out that there aren't any issues at home, that it is just the student's lack of caring, then it's time for her to go. In my contract, even when someone flakes and I have to kick her out, her fees have to be paid through the end of the year, as well as the fees for someone to step into her part.

We also have something in our contract about parental behavior. It touches upon the parent's responsibilities as a dance mom (or dad). Do the parents understand that when they go to a dance convention or competition and stay in a big fancy hotel or go to a football or hockey game where beer is being sold, it is against the rules to become intoxicated? When parents are intoxicated and publicly displaying poor or unsportsmanlike behavior, screaming and yelling, ripping on the coach or the other team's coach, that's not okay and it's against the commitment they have made to my studio. If they are representing the dance team or club, or if they are there because their child is competing or attending the event, they have to set a good example for my company and honor their commitment to me by behaving themselves.

When parents act out, yell, or become intoxicated, they're embarrassing and humiliating the organization, the teacher, and their own kids. At my studio, the entire family enters into an agreement with the dance studio. Parents and their children need to take it very seriously and keep their commitments.

Here are a few tips for teaching kids how to keep commitments:

- **Give them a task.** Even a toddler can learn to do things independently. This will help build confidence and encourage your child to venture into the world without fear. When children are older, have them set the table, babysit a younger sibling while you cook dinner, and tidy up their room.

- **Offer some choices.** I'm not saying allow your kids to pick candy and soda for breakfast. I'm saying give them two options: "Would you like cereal or toast?" and allow them to make the decision.

- **Stop doing things for them.** Hold back the helping hand. If you're always tying your child's shoelaces, do you think she'll ever learn how to do it herself?

- **Hold them accountable.** Tweens and teens especially crave independence. They don't want curfews or limitations. They want all the new cool tech toys without knowing how to care for them. So when you give them a new phone and they lose it (because they're kids and they will!), hold them responsible. Give them a quarter instead of another phone.

. . . .

Dear Abby:

I am thirteen and just beginning dance classes for the first time. I'm superflexible because I have been in gymnastics for five years. I really want to get to the competition level of dancing and do well. How can I become the best dancer I can be?

Although gymnastics and dance may seem similar, gymnastics is a sport, and dance is an art. Use your flexibility to enhance your dancing, but realize you have a long road ahead of you. You need to work in a turned-out position, rather than parallel, and your ballet training is the key to success.

Abby

. . . .

BATTLING BOREDOM, BAD SPORTSMANSHIP, AND OTHER REASONS KIDS WANT TO QUIT

Reign Dance Productions, home of the Abby Lee Dance Company, offers the best in dance education. We never let other children hold a child back. If your children are talented, we will constantly be challenging them. There is no need for them to move to another class. They may be encouraged to take private lessons, but the tap teacher is going to tell them to double-time that step, or do it with a wing, or add a pickup, while the other kids are just working on the step. My smartest or best kids in the class don't always go across the floor first. When they're really good, I'll make them go across the floor first as a demonstrator for the rest of the class, but using their weak side—the side that doesn't come naturally to them. This also helps to strengthen that side so they'll be strong on both sides. I'm constantly challenging my students, and there's not much chance they'll get bored when they're in my studio.

Sometimes kids become bored with school because it comes too easily. Maybe they need to be in another class, but it's a teacher's job to decide that. It is also the job of the coach to realize when a kid "has it" and would be more challenged at a different level. So maybe in terms of age, height, or weight, they need to compete at this level, but in terms of training they can work out with the older kids or veterans.

ALDC STUDIO ETIQUETTE

I am raising ladies and gentlemen, not trash. I expect certain rules to be observed in my studio. That goes for the moms as well . . .

- **Pull your own weight.** Don't wait for everyone to do things for you. If you're on a team, I expect you to do your part.

- **Be humble.** No one likes a kid who's full of herself. Being confident is one thing; being a stuck-up show-off is another entirely. All my girls better be supportive of one another. There is no one-upping. It makes me see red.

- **Stand up for yourself.** If you want a solo this week, come talk to me about it and tell me why. Don't send your mommy in to do your dirty work for you. I have a very strong rapport with my students. They know my door is always open to them, and I expect them to communicate to me any issues they're having.

I think kids quit when it's too difficult. As long as it's easy, they love it. Kids love what comes naturally. And the things that come naturally come easy to them. Children have to have that innate sense of competitiveness if they want to keep getting better. They compete against themselves every moment, whether it's in sports, dance, or academics.

When kids are bored, sometimes it has nothing to do with what you're teaching or asking. Sometimes they're just lazy. Or sometimes it stops being fun, and often it just doesn't come easy anymore and they have to work for it, but they don't want to.

When you first join something, it should be because you're interested in it and because it looks enticing. It should be something that looks fun, or seems like you would enjoy it, or maybe your girlfriends are all doing it, so you want to do it too (no pun intended). So you join, and maybe at first you're awkward. In dance, that's the kid who needs to stay in dance class because she's uncoordinated and has two left feet. Maybe she's feeling like a klutz because she trips all the time or she's pigeon-toed or has bad posture—these flaws will most definitely keep a child from winning a dance competition or becoming a pro, but a child who has any of these characteristics needs to be in dance class. She needs to work on her posture and her turnout. For the girls, they need to walk like a lady. They need to look in the mirror and be conscious of their posture and how they carry themselves. When you're in front of a mirror in a leotard, you're going to see where there are flaws; for example, are you swaybacked?

I think that dance is different from other activities because so many things have to be right about your body for you to truly become a great dancer. Find out if your kid really has what it takes to excel in any arena before you buy all the necessary gear. I can say that from experience. I was a Brownie and a Girl Scout. I took sewing at the Sears department store sewing school. I took ice-skating at the mall and moved from the red circles to the green. I took roller-skating lessons—turns out, I'm better on four wheels than on a blade. I danced one day a week like every other kid. I went to charm school. I played the clarinet. I did it all, because that's when the whole "well-rounded" thing was in for kids. I was even in the ski club. I went long enough in each activity to buy the outfit and all the accessories I needed, and then I would get tired of it, and my parents would say, "No, you made a commitment, so you have to keep going, but you don't have to do it again next year."

Eventually, I discovered that I was creative. I found out what I was destined for: bossing others around, being in charge, planning events, creating everything from the menus to the centerpieces to the entertainment. You name it, I can design the costumes, dress everyone around me, and shop for it all wholesale. I liked the creative aspects of this dance business, and the rest is history. So I think eventually kids find their niche and will be drawn to what is good for them and what they like. Be smart about it and make them follow through and honor their commitments. Make them continue until your contract is up or until the season is over. Never leave the team hanging.

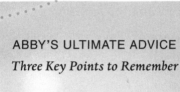

ABBY'S ULTIMATE ADVICE
Three Key Points to Remember

1. Teach your children that when they make a commitment, it is imperative that they follow through on it, no matter how much they object, cry, or try to convince you otherwise.

2. Commitments start with you, the parent. Lead by example, and your children will follow.

3. Don't fall into the trap of punishing your children by taking away things that are actually good for them (like dance).

It Takes Fifteen Years to
Make an Overnight Success

You're never a loser until you quit trying.
—*Mike Ditka*

CHILDREN USUALLY START DANCE at the age of three. If they put fifteen years in, then they'll be eighteen, graduate from high school, and have a complete dance education from my studio. They will have learned everything they need to know about this business. They will have all the right tools to go out and be successful, and hopefully, they will have learned some tricks of the trade along with some networking skills. Hopefully, they will have met the right people and stayed away from the wrong ones. They will be knowledgeable and they will be at the top of their game. That's what I mean when I say it takes fifteen years to make an overnight sensation.

In general, by the age of eight, you should be asking about your daughter, "Is she getting better at this?," and by eleven she should be getting serious. By the ages of thirteen, fourteen, and fifteen, she should already be broadening her skill set with an eye on becoming a professional dancer, archer, or world-class scientist. At sixteen or seventeen, she should be getting her name out there in her chosen field—networking by submitting articles to the local newspaper; making school officials aware of her by winning the national science fair. When it comes to performing, this means attending conventions, winning competitions, and earning scholarships—all so that she's ready, at the age of eighteen, for the big time, whether that means writing a novel, attending MIT, or landing her first Broadway show on the Great White Way.

People who are lucky are prepared when opportunity knocks. When you have an audition for the musical *Oklahoma!* you don't go out the night before and rent the movie. You think about all the steps I taught you when you were a kid and did that hoedown. You think about the big ballet scene and know it like the back of your hand. You've studied the original choreography; you remember routines you did as a youngster; you are prepared. You always have your nails and hair done. You are always ready for that agent to call and say you have an audition. In New York, you will most likely find out about an open-call audition online or in a trade publication like *Backstage*. It's usually at least a couple of days in advance. You're excited and you know where to go and what you're going to wear. In Los Angeles, it's typical for your agent to call you when the audition is literally within the hour. You have to be on top of your game and be prepared for anything at any time on the West Coast.

· ·

Dear Abby:
I really love to dance, but my family just can't afford dance
classes right now. What can I do at home to keep my dancing
skills up so that in the future when my family has enough
money, I won't be too far behind my peers?

Watch reruns *of Dance Moms* and *Abby's Ultimate Dance*
Competition and learn from the corrections given to others.
You can always become more flexible and stronger at
home for free. Something simple like splits for flexibility
and push-ups for strength. Try walking on your hands
all over the house. This will keep you in shape while you
aren't attending regular classes. Perhaps your family could
ask if they could clean the studio on the weekends, or do
something like editing music, or ordering costumes, or
maybe the owner of the studio needs a cleaning lady at
home. Whatever it takes, just do it.

Abby
· ·

PREPARING YOUR CHILD
FOR A CAREER IN DANCE

I think it should be a prerequisite for having children
that you will take them to see the Radio City Christmas
Spectacular and a Broadway show. Observe your children
during these performances to see if they're watching,
fidgeting, or falling asleep. If they are bored and yawn-

ing, then chances are they don't have a future in musical theater. There are so many kids in the world who dance, and so many parents who spend tons of money on costumes, rhinestones, and entering solo routines into dance competitions for their kids. They think nothing of spending hundreds of dollars for their diva dancer to get onstage in front of judges to win a trophy, but they would never think of spending hundreds of dollars on a ticket to a Broadway show. Most parents would never dream of going on vacation to New York City. How many shows can you pack into one weekend? I do it all the time. It's expensive, but if you don't patronize the theater, then who is going to want to pay to see your kid? How do you expect other people to want to come and spend money on a ticket when you don't?

I've taken my dancers to New York a million times for competitions and study trips throughout the thirty-three-year history of the ALDC. When I've gotten half-price tickets at TKTS for the hottest show, I share this information with my students. Most of them would rather take their parents' hard-earned money and go down the street to buy T-shirts than see a live performance. Yet all these kids, when asked in an interview what they wanted to be when they grow up, say they want to dance on Broadway.

Take your kids ice-skating on a Saturday afternoon before you sign them up for the ten-week session. See if they can even get up on their skates. If it's water-skiing, does your kid pop right up? If so, then go buy a boat. If your kid can't even drag the surfboard to the ocean, chances are he isn't going to be a surfer.

There are many ways to try to find out what your children can and can't do and where their talent lies before investing a huge amount of money and signing a contract. Every little girl dances around the living room. This doesn't necessarily mean they're all going to be prima ballerinas. Not by a long shot!

Another thing parents need to worry about is wearing their kids too thin. I know singing, acting, and dance are all quite necessary to call yourself a triple threat. I know football and track go hand in hand because if you play football and then you run track in the off-season, it makes you faster on the field. But if your kid plays soccer one season, and then she plays golf, and then she plays basketball, and then she swims, are you spreading her too thin? Shouldn't she really concentrate on overall fitness and conditioning in order to be the best soccer player she can be?

Parents also have to be careful which additional activities they sign their kids up for. Ballet in the winter and water ballet in the summer sounds like a plan. Swimming is usually the best exercise to lose weight and get in shape. However, swimming is the worst exercise for dancers because it works the wrong muscles in the wrong way. As a dancer you need to be able to jump into the air against gravity, where in swimming, you're floating.

For those kids who are naturally talented and have the gift of becoming great athletes, you need to be careful not to push them beyond their limits. I know one parent, a basketball coach, who had his daughter dribbling a ball with her right hand a hundred times and her left hand a hundred times each morning. She was only four years old. The child began to stutter. Her parents, clearly upset, headed to the pediatrician for some answers. Physically, everything checked out, so the doctor asked for her daily routine. Well, after hearing about the basketball practice, he quickly stopped Coach O. in his tracks and explained that she didn't have a dominant side, because her dad was having her work both left and right equally. Needless to say, his all-star was registered for dancing school the very next day. The closest she came to a half-court was as a cheerleader.

Every dancer has a good side, but when working with the well-trained ones, you will never be able to tell what side it is.

When is too much too much? I think parents should let their children lead the way, as far as what activities they want to try. They need to let their kids figure out what they're going to be good at and how much time they want to invest, and as I previously mentioned, some kids just get it and others don't.

. . . .

Dear Abby:

My mom is always pushing me to be the best dancer in the studio although my teacher always says I'm one of her best dancers. My mom is driving me crazy! What should I do?

Perhaps you should sit down with your mom and explain that if you were always the best at everything, then continuing to take lessons to learn would be pointless. It's good to have other dancers to look up to and to challenge yourself.

Abby

. . . .

YOUR KIDS DESERVE THE VERY BEST

Finding the best teacher for your child is important. I've said it before but I'll say it again: investigate your child's teachers or coaches the way you would a pediatrician. Dance teachers don't need a license, unlike a hairdresser or even a dog groomer. Nobody has a say over what I teach or what I do. A health inspector doesn't visit my studio. Any hands-on activity like teaching dance should be carefully selected.

Be sure to check out the facility. Is it conducive to the training? In our case, the floors are specifically designed for dance and they are Equity approved. If it's a track, is it made of the right materials? Is it clay, dirt, or what? What is the facility like? Does all the equipment look up-to-date and top-of-the-line? Is everything up to your standards as a parent?

Your children are entitled to the very best. Why not give it to them? Maybe they're not going to do it forever, but if you're paying money, why take them to a glorified babysitter? Why not take them where they can get a formal education?

There are kids who come to my studio for a year or five and they don't end up being dancers, but they got what they paid for, a dance education. They had qualified, certified instructors who knew what they were doing. They had opportunities to get onstage and perform. They even had bus trips to see alumni in various productions.

Are the instructors themselves continuing their own education? Do they attend classes? Do they attend conferences and seminars? Are they constantly upgrading their teaching techniques? Dance is an ever-evolving, constantly changing art form. Is this studio changing with the times or are they still doing jazz from 1978?

COMPLEMENTARY ANGLES
by Mark McCormick

Raising kids today is a whole lot different from when we grew up. Growing comes more from the mistakes you make than from all of the exciting victories, and parents today don't let their kids fail—ever. Both Abby's parents and mine were part of a different generation, solid middle-class people who worked hard, had perfect credit, and wanted more for their children than they had for themselves when they were growing up. Our dads both enjoyed nice cars, a round of golf with the guys, and regular games of gin rummy at Alcoma Golf Club. Our mothers found solace in their Catholic upbringing, while they worked, raised children, and contributed to the PTA all with one hand tied behind their backs.

Supposedly, we met as toddlers in the kiddie pool, but it wasn't until tenth grade when our geometry teacher, Mr. Roman, thought it would be a great idea if the guy that sat in front of Abby—ugh, lucky me, McCormick—went over to her house and helped her figure out why two complementary angles are as easy as pie! It is crystal clear today why school wasn't Abby's thing; she had somewhere more exciting to be and something else more interesting she could have been doing. We've had a lot of laughs, many intelligent conversations, and a few brilliant ideas throughout the years, yet too much time always passes in between. Fortunately, Abby made some good choices along the way. She had to be tough and strong, and she's all the better for it now.

As we enter this next chapter of our lives, I am so amazed by what she has accomplished. I was there at the start, back when they only gave out first-, second-, and third-place trophies. I remember how hard the struggle was and how sad the defeat. That is what makes this success all the sweeter. Enjoy it, Abby! You deserve all the wonderful things that are coming your way.

and the Winner is...

DANCE EDUCATORS OF AMERICA
...ALL FRY MISS DEA 2010

CHLOE LUKASIAK

1988
TEEN MISS DANCE OF AMERICA

KATIE HACKETT

Abby Lee Dance Company
Reigns Supreme!

1995 MISS DANCE OF PA

HEATHER SNYDER

abby lee
DANCE COMPANY

1997 JR. MISS DANCE OF PA

RACHEL KREILING

Amer

Abby Goes Hollywood

Abby's Ultimate Dance Competition
Seasons 1 & 2

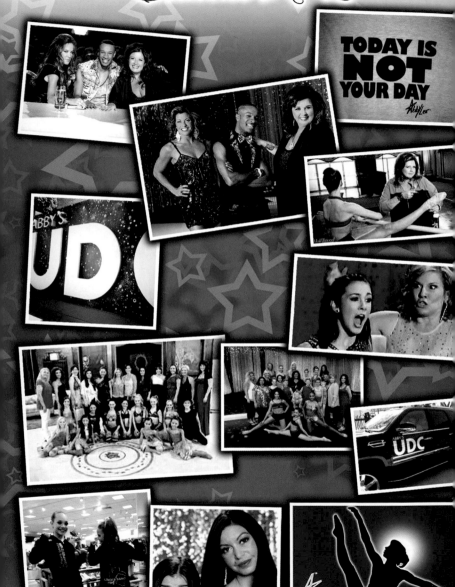

Broadway Baby
My Very Best Friend

"Baby in a Box"
My Very Best Work
Original Cast, 1999
Revival Cast, 2009

DANCE MOMS

Premiered July 13, 2011
& We've Been in Your Living Rooms Ever Since
Dance Moms Celebrated Its 100th Episode
April 15, 2014. Thank You for Watching!

DANCE MOMS

THE MANIAC IS BACK.
DANCE MOMS

DANCE MOMS

SHE MAKES STARS, NOT FRIENDS.
DANCE MOMS
Lifetime

GUEST JUDGE
ABBY LEE MILLER
TONIGHT 8/7c abc

Danceteacher
The Real
Abby Lee Miller

TUESDAYS 9.8c
Abby's
ULTIMATE DANCE
COMPETITION

DANCE MOMS
JUNE 4TH TUESDAY
lifetime

PITTSBURGH
DANCE MOMS
MANY PRINCESSES. ONE QUEEN.
JUNE XXth 9PM
lifetime
your life. your time.

All the Success in the World Is Meaningless Without Someone to Share It With!

Mark McCormick is an old friend and the vice president of Abby Lee Apparel. He oversees the development, production, and distribution of all logo wear. Mark is also the general manager in the Sporto Division.

DEALING WITH ENVIOUS FRIENDS, MOMS, AND TEACHERS WHO JUST DON'T GET IT

Dance isn't recognized in public schools like football games on Friday night, and there are no letterman sweaters. Your classmates at school may wonder why you're not a varsity cheerleader or on the school's dance team or in the high school musical when you're this hotshot dancer, acrobat, or gymnast. They don't get it. But there is something you can do to help: invite your friends to come to the dance studio to watch what you do. And if you're dead sure you're going to win a competition, then invite your friends from school, pay their admission fees, and have your mother go pick them up so they can see what you do. That will give them a whole new respect for you and your dancing.

I urge you to entertain your teachers as well. If there is a talent show at school or in the community, sign up! Show them how talented you really are. One of my professional dancers who performed in the *Beauty and the Beast* show at Walt Disney World's Hollywood Studios in Orlando, Florida, was in the talent show at her school every year. She never wanted to participate, but her dad forced her to take part. He was a celebrated math teacher in the high school. He wanted his little girl to get the recognition she deserved. He was a smart guy who had a long-term plan. When his graceful girl graduated, not one principal, guidance counselor, or teacher gave her a hard time about pursuing a dance career before college.

And that's with everything, not just dance. It could be bringing your friends from school to your piano recital or golf tournament. Let them see for themselves what it is you dedicate so much of your time to—don't try to teach them. And if they don't respect what you do and don't understand that you can't go to the sleepover because you have early morning or weekend commitments, then they aren't really your friends.

Not getting it and envy are two different things. Let's break that down. You can still have fun with people who don't get it. You can have your neighborhood friends, friends in other activities, and school friends. This way you always have someone to go to a Sadie Hawkins dance with. You always have someone to trick-or-treat with, because you can call anyone a good friend. As far as envy goes, never compromise your own dream because you are frightened of someone mocking you, of someone causing you unnecessary stress.

At the Abby Lee Dance Company, one of our students started dancing when she was older, and she didn't have a lot of time to commit because she worked. She was inexperienced because she didn't walk in at four years old, and she didn't know any dance history, but she worked really hard. That kid doesn't have good legs, good feet, or good flexibility, but what she does have is a *brain*. She picks up choreography quickly. On the flip side, you could be book smart and get straight As and take all the accelerated classes, but when it comes to comprehensive choregraphy and learning an entire routine overnight, you fail.

I think there are envious people everywhere, and I tell my students all the time that when the envious people quit talking about you, that's when you need to start worrying. Girls are mean, that's a fact! Girls are going to be nasty, and they want what they can't have. If you "have it," that's when envy comes into play. It's an ugly disease, yet it's everywhere. People can ruin their lives by being envious of others. People try to make other people's lives really difficult when envy sets in.

You have to let the haters hate and turn the other cheek and stick your nose up in the air while continuing the journey on the road to success. There will always be a lot of envious people, and the tougher your skin can be, and the more you can blow those people off and not give them an ounce of credibility, the better off you'll be.

It's tough. I don't like having to tell a ten-year-old girl to watch her back because there is a grown person who's nasty and bitter and envious of her success, but sometimes I have to.

. . . .

Dear Abby:

My daughter has been taking ballet for seven years now and absolutely loves it. The problem is, she is now fixated on losing weight, thinking this will improve her ballet. She wants to be a "skinny" ballerina. She is well within a normal weight for her size and age, and we're worried she is going to develop an eating disorder with this kind of thinking. What should we do?

Contrary to popular belief, eating disorders do not originate from dance class, gymnastics, or skating. There's usually a deep-rooted self-esteem issue such as not wanting to grow up, to develop, or to get your period. (Sadly, some of the most talented people are obsessed with the idea of being perfect. When they look in the mirror, they only see imperfections, so little by little they slip away.) Sometimes parents don't want to admit there is a problem. Trust your coach; coaches usually see the signs before Mom and Dad do. There's also not wanting to have the responsibility of driving a car, of being independent, or of making decisions. Or perhaps the child is in a family where she's never been allowed to make a decision. She doesn't pick out her own clothes. She doesn't get to choose what she's going to do today or where she's going—her parents control everything. Maybe the only thing she can control is what goes into her mouth or what comes out. Perhaps she is starving for attention. I think it's important for your daughter to have some role models who are thicker and stronger and healthier-looking ballerinas. Investigate professional companies such as ABT and New York City Ballet. Find some dancers who are taller, broader, and stronger. Get videos and pictures of them. Buy her posters, so she can see that the too skinny, emaciated look has gone away for good.

Abby

. . . .

BALANCING DANCE AND SCHOOLWORK

There are so many more alternative ways of educating your child today than were available when I was a kid. You need to gather information and investigate your options. I think a lot of time is wasted at school—waiting in line to get on the bus, and then riding the bus home, and stopping at every neighborhood along the way. Waiting in line to go to the cafeteria, buying your lunch, eating your lunch, and giggling with your girlfriends.

A big story line on *Dance Moms* this season has been about Melissa's choice to homeschool her children, Maddie and Mackenzie. Well, let me say my piece. I grew up in Pennsylvania and I am a firm believer in our public education system. However, we have a very strict attendance policy in our public schools. Take it from the kid who grew up with allergies and asthma, who had bronchitis for all of September and October one year, and got to school late with Vicks VapoRub still on her chest. The policy is: thirty days absent and you fail. How would Maddie and Mackenzie, these exemplary students, fly to L.A. to audition for a movie? How would they spend weeks recording a CD? And how would they take additional classes that their school doesn't offer?

Also, nobody is letting Melissa teach her children anything, not even Men 101. When I pitched the idea of an alternative education for Maddie and Mackenzie, I proposed that Melissa take the girls to the Carnegie library daily. Have a Carnegie Mellon University computer-engineering major teach them math, science, and computer lessons. Then have a scholarship student from Spain teach them Spanish and another from Japan instruct them in Japanese. Obviously, a professor from the renowned musical-theater program would teach them history and English, and give acting lesson too.

On the other hand, academic professors say that from kindergarten through fifth grade, every kid should attend school so they learn how to stand in line at the water fountain, how to go through the lunch line, and how to put things back where they found them. This is where they learn how to get along well with others. You learn all of these important things in school, just like in the baby class at dancing school.

If your kid is going to a traditional public or private school, take time to figure out if he or she is in the right class. Did the AP Calculus teacher happen to see your daughter in the hallway and ask her to join his class because he thinks she has what it takes? Does this scenario ring a bell? Did you, as the parent, call the guidance counselor and request that your daughter be placed in the AP Calculus class? If your child takes four hours to do her homework each night, she's in the wrong class, because the curriculum was designed for a child who can handle that class. Someone who would only take thirty minutes to do the same homework.

Some of the kids at my studio are homeschooled and some attend the Cyber Charter School, which is an online educational program. I have a recent graduate who's nineteen and he was cyberschooled. Things got bad for him when he was in junior high and had a medical issue. It was much easier for him to sit at a computer in the comfort of his home. It made more sense in his case. Now he's on Broadway in the cast of *Newsies*, doing eight shows a week.

As far as balancing their education with dance, you would find that most overachievers and perfectionists do it all. If they're really on the ball at dance, then they're generally on the ball academically as well. If they're lazy, they simply aren't going to do it. I think time management, which their parents should teach them, is important.

Do the mothers have a job, a husband, children, get supper on the table, get the kids where they need to be, and make cupcakes for the next day? It's up to parents to teach their children good work ethics and responsibility. If you live it, then your children will learn it. I guarantee it!

. . . .

Dear Abby:

I'm twelve years old and all I want to do is dance, but my parents want me to take lots of other lessons, like piano and tennis. How can I convince them not to make me do that???

I would figure out some way to outsmart your parents. Bang on that piano as loud as you can early in the morning and late at night. And there's only so many times you can forget your tennis racket before the coach is going to tell your mom and dad that he or she doesn't want you as a student. So drive with your mom all the way to practice, get out, and announce that you forgot your racket or tennis shoes or whatever it is you need to play. The coach is going to say, "She's not serious, we don't want her here," and then you'll be free to dance.

Don't get me wrong—I think there are a variety of activities out there that can make you a better dancer. Playing piano is helpful for your dancing because it teaches you musicality and teaches you how to read sheet music and understand the music you're dancing to better. You might want to squeeze in a piano lesson once a week. If you want to excel in dance, then my advice is to avoid sports that work against you. Track-and-field activities make your feet go straight ahead, which works against your turnout and this goes against what you're trying to do in ballet class. Long-distance running is hard on the knees too. Stick to sports that are educational and that you can do for the rest of your life, such as golf.

Abby

. . . .

ABBY'S ULTIMATE ADVICE
Three Key Points to Remember

1. Luck is that place where preparation meets opportunity. Work hard and be prepared when opportunity comes knocking—it may be a while before it comes back for another visit!

2. Start your kids in dance young, and help them find their passion. Encourage them to dream big dreams, and give them the tools they need to pursue them.

3. Find the best dance instructor and the best dance studio for your child—don't settle for second best (or worse).

GRANDE FINALE

You're Only as Good as Your Last Performance

I believe that tomorrow is another day and I believe in miracles.

—*Audrey Hepburn*

I WISH I HAD a crystal ball and could tell the future like Zoltar in the Tom Hanks film *Big*—or like the fortune-teller who read my aura at that charity event a bunch of years ago—but I don't, and I can't. I do know that I've worked very hard to get where I am today, and that's not going to stop anytime soon. I have even bigger plans for the future, and I can't wait to see how everything turns out five, ten, and twenty years from now.

There's one thing I do know for sure: I don't want to die in Pittsburgh.

Nobody wants to die in Pittsburgh. I cannot die in Pittsburgh and that's the honest-to-God truth. I can't go down that way. So when I look ahead to my own future, I see myself doing something that will take me to another part of the country. For example, I would like to design dance costumes for the masses, and also design a line of children's clothing. I see myself living in Orlando or Miami, or even in Los Angeles—wherever the work takes me. I know that the place I eventually move to has got to be hot and sunny. If I want snow I'll go to Steamboat Springs, Aspen, or someplace where it's white and pretty—not gray, dirty, and slushy like the stuff I pay to have removed from my parking lot.

I cannot believe that I'll be fifty soon. I have a while before I hit that frightening number, but it's astonishing to me that I have been on this earth that long. I just hope I accomplish what I was put here on this earth to do. I feel I'm working on it, and I will continue to always do more and do it better.

I love the idea of having a talk show called *Abby Said!* I hate to drop names, but I'm starting with Robert Redford and Barbra Streisand—on the same day on the same couch together. That would be surreal. Of course I would book Tom Cruise and John Travolta, providing they would do their signature moves on the show. I need to see John Travolta do that walk from *Saturday Night Fever* in the flesh and Tom Cruise slide across the stage in his underwear doing his routine from *Risky Business*.

I wouldn't book too many women, but Whoopi Goldberg would be a definite must, along with Broadway babes like Chita Rivera and Ann Reinking. I would want to interview Ben Affleck and Matt Damon together but without their wives. I want the scoop, the real dirt on what happened. And I would have lots of people from the dance industry.

One thing I've discovered is that it's a big wide world out there. I've been to Elton John's Oscar-viewing party three years running and the Tony Awards three times as well. I've also been to the *American Idol* finals, the Teen Choice Awards, and the Emmys. Next on my list is the Grammys, and any other award show I can get into.

That's been a perk of the show that's been huge. All the fans are taking photos of all the celebrities, and the celebrities want to take *my* picture because *their* kids watch the show. I have to give a shout-out to Jennifer Lawrence— congrats on your Oscar! On the red carpet going in for the awards ceremony she mentioned *Dance Moms*.

I would also like to work toward getting dance back into the schools. It's no secret that performing arts programs—from drama, to music, to dance—have been severely cut back or killed altogether because of budget concerns. Today everything is about getting the best test scores possible—the academics. But there's more to life than academics, and cutting back on the arts is, I believe, doing a huge disservice to our children and to the future of our nation.

I think every child should dance, boys and girls, whether they're in private or public school. I think some kids learn differently and you get exceptional kids in the arts, and to cut all these programs, we're going to miss out on youngsters who could have been great. They'll end up frustrated artists with dead-end jobs with no hope of living out their passion in life. They'll be doing something they hate when they should have been doing something they *love*.

In America, most kids have a lot of freedom to choose what they want to do, and often they choose the wrong thing. They waste time and money, and end up being a failure even though Mom and Dad tell them that they're fantastic. The kid who's born with a perfect dancer's body who should be a dancer may want to play soccer. That kid probably isn't going to end up supporting his family as a professional soccer player. He'll end up doing something else when he could have been a great dancer.

I think it's important to keep the dance programs in school, and for every child to learn how to dance and to experience live theater—to go to a show where people are performing onstage. It's an education that will pay off for years to come, and it just might lead to the career of a lifetime.

Wherever my future takes me, I know that success will follow. How can I be so certain? Because I always set my barre high and I refuse to give up and I will never back down. I will work harder than anyone else, fight harder than anyone else, and reach higher than anyone else—that's one thing I can guarantee. It's just the way my parents raised me, and I'm not going to change anytime soon.

Something one of my best students, Katie Hackett, said about me sticks close to my heart. She said, "Everything that Abby wanted for all of us has happened for her."

It's always been about my students, about turning

them into accomplished dancers who could get a job at the highest levels of the profession. My own success is a reflection of their success. As I see my students go on to exciting, lucrative careers on the stage, and on television and in films, I know that I have done everything that I can do to help them along the way. I'm proud of them, and I hope they are now proud of me.

It's true: everything that I have ever wanted for my students is now happening to me. I can't wait to see what tomorrow brings for all of us!

I want all of my students to buy this book, but there are a few things I'd rather they didn't know.

The first would be that I fell asleep while seeing Elvis live and in person. This wasn't some corny Elvis impersonator at some rinky-dink county fair; no this was THE Elvis Presley, in person in Las Vegas. We went to this swanky supper club that seats a thousand people. Of course my dad, the big spender, tipped the maître d' way too much money so that we could get a table right down in front. I was about seven or eight years old and I certainly knew who Elvis was because of all his classics, which I'd heard at dancing school. "Blue Suede Shoes," "Jailhouse Rock," and "Hound Dog" held my interest for a while, but I think the hours spent in the hot desert sun combined with the heavy dose of chlorine from an afternoon dip in the pool took the swivel right out of my hips. After a few too many Shirley Temples, I had my head flat down on the table and was sound asleep.

Now, if this had been one of my students, and her parents had paid a fortune for her ticket and she wasn't watching every pelvic thrust the living legend did, I would have made her do a hundred push-ups, write a report on the evening's events, and stand up to sing "Burning Love" in front of the class.

The next night, my parents weren't making the same mistake. They took me to see Debbie Reynolds's nightclub act, and it was extra special because one of my mom's former students, Albert Stephenson, was a dancer in the show. Seeing him perform is why we flew all that way; he was our excuse to go to Vegas in the first place. I remember how funny and fabulous Debbie was, and how dashing and debonair Albert was. He looked at my mom like she was *the bomb*. I saw the respect and admiration in his eyes, and I took note of the kind and gentle way he treated her.

My mom had lots of male students in Miami, and they all seemed to be extremely successful. Albert was one of those employable dancers. While he was dancing on Broadway in the show *Liza with a "Z,"* he was often photographed by the paparazzi coming out of Studio 54 with Liza on his arm. He went on to do many shows. One of my favorites was *A Day in Hollywood/A Night in the Ukraine*. He also took on the job of choreographer. My mom was so proud of him when he was working on the TV special *Night of 100 Stars*.

My connection to Albert led to many starstruck moments in my life. The first one happened immediately

after the Debbie Reynolds show was over. We were ushered backstage to meet the cast and hopefully to have a
photo taken with Miss Debbie. Albert arranged for my
mom and dad to go with some of the dancers over to
another opulent hotel on the Strip to see the *Lido de Paris*
show. This was a standard showgirl revue, which meant
it was topless—no kids. What would they do with poor
little Abby? No problem! She will stay here in the pent-
house suite reserved for the hotel's headliner and Debbie
Reynolds will babysit!

The second thing that I'd prefer my students didn't
know would have to be the secret that I have held on to
since it happened, until now. I hope this particular dance
mom will be forgiving when she reads this. Here goes
nothing.

A cool, crisp winter day had me driving to New York
City with Sandy and a bunch of kids. The kids outnum-
bered the seat belts in my Cadillac. So one of the very gen-
erous moms (whom I will call Barb) lent me her minivan.
It wasn't exactly my style, but what the heck. We got to
New York with no problem. The kids were all safely in
dance class, and Sandy and I headed to the garment district to find fabric, appliques, and probably feathers too.
While we were there, we got a parking ticket for not having a noncommercial vehicle parked on Thirty-Eighth
Street between Eighth and Ninth Avenues. We didn't
want to get another ticket, so I had a brilliant idea. I called
one of the young, unemployed dancers who happened to

live with some of my employed professional dancers and asked her to come help us out. She was going to sit in the driver's seat of the van, and if a cop came, she would just drive around the block. Well, our lookout never looked behind her, and sure enough, an officer walked right up to the back of the van and wrote us another ticket.

Risk taker that I am, I figured that we'd already been given two parking tickets in two hours, so it couldn't get any worse. We'd leave the tickets on the windshield and if anybody else came along, they'd see that we'd already been fined. That's not exactly what happened . . . They towed the minivan!

So we had to tromp all the way down to the impound lot where they had this woman's vehicle captive until we paid the fines to get it out. Well, this is where the story really gets good. We didn't have the registration card, and we didn't know the license-plate number. We didn't know the make or the model. For Pete's sake, we couldn't even remember what color the van was! At this point, we had two choices: laugh or cry. We took the high road and started to giggle uncontrollably. The kind of laughing fit you have in church. We tried to contain ourselves as we strolled through the massive garage filled with hundreds of cars, pressing the remote-control car keys. Simple plan: when we heard it beep and saw the lights flash, we would have found the correct vehicle. But the gig is up. When Barb reads this she might recall the odd phone calls she received from us, asking questions about her minivan.

Every ALDC trip is educational. What did we learn from this experience? In New York, it's cheaper to have your car impounded than it is to pay for parking!

As an adult role model, I always want to appear in control. I want my students to feel safe in my presence. I hope they look to me with confidence and pride, and think, "That's my dance teacher; she's not taking any crap from anybody." I want the boys I train to be perfect gentlemen and the girls to be empowered women who stand up for themselves.

That's why the third thing that I don't want anyone to know is that I am deathly afraid of heights. I guess it all started when I was a little kid at the swimming pool with my dad. That ladder to the high dive went straight up in the air, perpendicular to the ground. I had to climb that ladder rung by rung. My dad was a volunteer with the swim team at our country club from around 1973 to 1976. And he remained active in planning and executing the Memorial Day opening weekend and the Labor Day closing festivities for many years after that. He loved the watermelon war, the coin toss, and of course the relay races. So diving off the high dive was kind of a no-brainer . . . for him! I think this is where my fear first started.

I also freak out at the mall when little ones stick their heads through the railing to look over the balcony. I would never ride a Ferris wheel. I'm okay in an elevator, unless it's made of glass so that you can look out and see the ground—that's where I imagine plummeting to my death. I'm not one to easily step right onto a moving escalator either. When I was a little girl, I tumbled from the top of one all the way to the bottom. I spent years after that searching for the elevator tucked back in the corner of department stores. Even to this day, I have to give it two or three tries before I muster up the courage to take that step onto the escalator. I fear falling all the time. I know what it feels like to dislocate a kneecap. It feels like your knee flies across the room ripping every muscle and tendon in its path and you crumble to the ground screaming in agony. That was my experience anyway. Inside an airplane, I'm perfectly comfortable. Outside on the wing, I would panic. No aerial acrobatics for this choreographer. My head make be in the clouds, but my feet are planted firmly on the ground.

NATIONAL TITLE HOLDERS

Dance Educators of America—National Title Holders

National Mr. Dance—Mark Myars

National Miss Dance—Asmeret Ghebremichael

National Junior Miss Dance—Allie Meixner

National Junior Miss Dance—Jennine Wedge

National Teen Miss Dance—Allie Meixner

National Young Sr. Miss Dance—Ashley Kacvinsky

National Young Sr. Miss Dance—Allie Meixner

National Miss Dance—Ashley Kacvinsky

National Young Sr. Miss Dance—Jennine Wedge

National Miss Dance—Amanda Stelluto

National Small Fry Mr. Dance—Izumi Presberry

National Teen Miss Dance—Chelsea Shott

National Mr. Dance—Jesse Johnson

National Sr. Miss Dance—Jessica Ice

National Small Fry Dance—Chloe Lukasiak

National Teen Miss Dance—Brittany Pent

National Miss Dance—Stephanie Pittman

National Miss Pre-Teen Dance—Brooke Hyland

National Small Fry Dance—Maddie Ziegler

National Miss Dance—Brittany Pent

National Teen Miss Dance—Payton Ackerman

National Mr. Dance—John Fiumara

And Over 40 Regional Title Winners

Dance Masters of America—National Title Holders

1992 Petite Miss Dance of America—Katie Hackett

1993 Teen Mr. Dance of America—Mark Myars

1994 National Capezio Excellence Scholarship Recipient—Mark Myars

1995 Junior Miss Dance of America—Katie Hackett

1996 National Capezio Excellence Scholarship Recipient—Mark Myars

1998 Teen Miss Dance of America—Katie Hackett

2000 Petite Miss Dance of America—Brittany Markle

2002 Junior Miss Dance of America—Brittany Markle

2002 National Algy. Excellence Scholarship Recipient—Brittany Markle

2008 National Excellence Overall Scholarship Recipient—John Fiumara

2009 Teen Mr. Dance of America—John Fiumara

2010 National Excellence Overall Scholarship Recipient—John Fiumara

2011 Mr. Dance of America—John Fiumara

West Coast Dance Explosion National Finals

2000 National Sr. Miss West Coast—Katie Hackett

2000 National Teen Miss West Coast—Semhar Ghebremichael

2006 National Jr. Mr. West Coast—John Fiumara

2008 National Teen Elite Dancer of the Year—Miranda Maleski

2010 National Sr. Elite Dancer of the Year—Miranda Maleski

Sheer Talent—National Title Holders

2013 Miss Dance—Nina Linhart

2013 Miss Small Wonder—Brooke Kosinski

Hollywood Vibe—National Dancers of the Year

2013 Junior Dancer of the Year—Brooke Kosinski

Starbound National Championship

2012 Teen Miss Starbound—Katherine Narasimhan

New York City Dance Alliance National Finale

1995 Outstanding Dancer of the Year—Mark Myars

Petite Miss Dance of Pennsylvania

1991—Stefi Schlarman	1999—Brittany Markle
1993—Katie Hackett	2008—Haley Greico
1995—Semhar Ghebremichael	2009—Maddie Ziegler
1998—Allie Meixner	

Junior Miss/Mr. Dance of Pennsylvania

1983—J. T. Shontz	1995—Katie Hackett
1991—Mark Myars	1997—Rachel Kreiling
1992—Erin Murphy	1999—Koree Kurkowski
1993—Stefi Schlarman	2000—Allie Meixner

2001—Brittany Markle

2004—Kaitlyn Reiser

2007—Nina Linhart

2009—Brooke Hyland

2009—Nick Dobbs

2011—Chloe Lukasiak

Teen Miss/Mr. Dance of Pennsylvania

1994—Michelle Pampena

1995—Stefi Schlarman

1997—Katie Hackett

1998—Semhar Ghebremichael

1999—Rachel Kreiling

2000—Ashley Kacvinsky

2001—Koree Kurkowski

2002—Allie Meixner

2003—Brittany Markle

2004—Crystal Jennings

2007—John Fiumara

2008—Jesse Johnson

2009—Brittany Pent

2011—Brandon Pent

Miss/Mr. Dance of Pennsylvania

1988—J. T. Shontz

1992—Jennifer Snyder

1995—Heather Snyder

1996—Mark Myars

1998—Asmeret Ghebremichael

2000—Katie Hackett

2001—Semhar Ghebremichael

2002—Ira Cambric

2004—Allie Meixner

2006—Jennine Wedge

2007—Crystal Jennings

2008—Amanda Stelluto

2009—Kaitlyn Reiser

2011—Nina Linhart

2011—John Fiumara

ARE YOU MOM ENOUGH?
How Well Do You Handle Losing?

Answer the following questions truthfully. Then see how you rate.

1. You buy a Lotto ticket and miss the jackpot by one number. You:

   A. Scream, curse, and shove the ticket down the trash compactor.
   B. Buy a ticket for next week. There's always tomorrow!
   C. Blame your husband for picking the wrong numbers. What the hell is wrong with him?

2. Another mom is chosen to be class parent. You:

   A. Send her a nasty e-mail—how dare that bitch steal your job!
   B. Congratulate her and ask if there's anything you can do to help.
   C. Demand a recount of the vote. Someone stuffed that ballot box!

3. Your neighbor's kid is playing Snow White in the elementary school play and your daughter got cast as Dopey. You:

   A. Switch schools: clearly they don't recognize talent when they see it.
   B. Sew her an adorable dwarf costume and tell her how proud of her you are.
   C. Ask the teacher how much money it took to make that loser's runt the lead.

4. You play a round of tennis with your BFF and she kicks your butt. You:

   A. Hurl your racket at her head.
   B. Offer to buy her lunch—she deserves it.
   C. Insist that the tennis pro check your racket, your sneakers, and the net. Clearly, something is amiss!

5. Your little sister just announced that she's gotten a huge job promotion. You're a stay-at-home mom. You:

   A. Call her office and make sure they know what they're in for—your sis is way too young for so much responsibility!
   B. Send her flowers and a congrats card.
   C. Scream at your husband and kids for getting you into this situation.

   If you answered mostly As:
   A little bitter, are we? Do you think pitching a fit and throwing furniture is going to get you anywhere? Have you met Cathy?

   If you answered mostly Bs:
   You are a graceful and gracious loser. You appreciate that it's not always about winning, it's how you play the game. Kudos for your self-control.

   If you answered mostly Cs:
   Have you looked in the mirror lately? Because there's the person who's really to blame. Stop shrugging off the responsibility for your shortcomings and you won't lose so often.

STANDING OVATION
Acknowledgments

I've got a lot of people to thank, starting with that girl I hit over the head with a baton in second grade when she didn't perform the correct choreography I had taught her for my weekly revue in the garage. If it wasn't for her, I probably would never have found my calling as a choreographer.

The Powers family, the Murphys, Diana Corbett, the Solaniks, the Pampenas, the Snyders, the Earleys, Rich Erdelyi, Stephanie Wedge, the Kreilings, the Litmans, Mary Stelluto, Lisa and J. T. Shontz, Laini Samuels, Linda Cravy Williams, Cindy Rohm, the Taorminas, and the Ices.

John and Marilyn Haack, Joanne King, Nancy Shubert, Gibby and Henrietta Goodworth, Karen and John Tobias, Graham, and Gary.

Andrew Para, Rachael Thoma Dennison, Gianna Martello, Jennine Wedge, James Washington, Kerra Alexander, Matt Saffron, Michelle Pampena, Colleen Sherer, Kelsey Keller, Auriel Welty, Deb and Elissa Berardi, Olivia Ice, Shannon Pratt, Emma Neal, Melissa Bowman, Sherri Markel, John Cunningham, Michael Cerniglia, Kim Martello, Patti Fiumara, Holly Frazier, Jill Vertes, and Melissa Gisoni.

Gil Stroming, John Crutchman, Alan Sherfield, Linda Diamond, Joe Lanteri, Vickie Sheer, Sheer Talent, Kevin, Alex, Dustin, Gary Pate, Ray Leeper, Anthony Morigerato, Doug Caldwell, Rowena Costumes, Cicci's, Joffrey Ballet, Richie Jackson, Robin Antin, Kevin Manno, Rachelle Rak, Michael Rooney, A. C. Ciulla, Eileen Grace, Andrew Logan, Raj Kapoor, MSA, and CTA.

Kathy Nickel McFaden, David Markman, Greenburg/Traurig, Todd Christopher, the Gersh Agency, Don Calaiaro, David Valencik, Suchir Batras, Ed Medvene, Dr. Robert Crossey, and Dr. Valerie Paul.

Jerry Ross, Mindy Rossi-Stabler, John Culbertson, Cookie Ramos, Michelle Rogers, Mark McCormick, Lori Kutch, Robert DiDiano, Terry Flaherty, Robin Dawn Ryan, Melissa Stokes, Darni Fenerty, Michele Larkin, R. J. Mitchell, Joanne and Barry Chapman, Sharon Howard, Becky Smitley, Rosanne Slifko, Lucy Mudrick, Ruby Daugherty, and Johnathan Hoffman.

Jane and Marcus Buckingham, Robert and Rosanna Chafino, Gino and Carrie Bonaroti, Amanda and Justin Chang, Jenny Kim and Frederick Beddingfield III, Brad Krevoy, and Rob Fox.

Lifetime network: Tim Nolan, Michael Padula, Linda Medvene, Kim Chesler, Mary Donahue, Rob Sharenow, Gena McCarthy, Tara Pietri, Nancy Dubuc, Aaron Day, Aaron Goldman, Richard McClaren, Jeff Collins, Collins Ave. Productions, Lesley Bandy, Sandi Johnson, Michael Hammond, all the Hammonds, Bryan Stinson, Dianna Kazandjidan, Andy Villalobos, Woody Lighting, Chip, Adesa, Jimmy Chriss, Adam Bultler, Carlos Palmer, Scott Shatsky, and the assistant director Theresa Moio.

HarperCollins: Lisa Sharkey, Tessa Woodward, Peter Economy, Dale Rohrbaugh, Mary Schuck, Lynn Grady, Lisa Stokes, Nyamckyc Waliyaya, Liate Stehlik, and Carly Bornstein.

Chris Hoye, Alissa Panichella, Tim Baudier, Portraits with Pride, Donna at Kinkos, the Dirty "O," Napoli's Pizza, and Pricilla My Twitter Girl.

Happiness is not something you find, but something you create . . . many thanks to each and every one of my Illustrious Alumni, Loyal Students, and their Supportive Parents who never caused any problems and always paid on time.

CURTAIN CALL
About Abby Lee Miller

Abby Lee Miller is the owner and director of the Maryen Lorrain Dance Studio in Pittsburgh. In May of 1995, she opened the doors to her brand-new state-of-the-art facility, renamed Reign Dance Productions. Ms. Miller founded the Abby Lee Dance Company in 1980 at the ripe old age of fourteen.

Ms. Miller was certified to teach by Dance Masters of America and received her twenty-five-year pin in 2011. In addition, she has been a consultant to several public school districts and was an adviser to *Dancer* magazine. She is honored to be a past president of Dance Masters of Pennsylvania. She has been the teacher and choreographer of sixty state and regional title holders and thirty national title winners!

Ms. Miller is a current member of Dance Educators of America and teaches master classes across the United

States. She is a sought-after adjudicator—invited to judge dance competitions throughout the United States and Canada. When time permits, Ms. Miller coaches top-notch dancers and critiques and corrects their solo performances. She currently operates ALDC Dance Off, an online dance competition where dancers submit their solo routines via the Internet and Ms. Miller gives them feedback, comments, and corrections.

A teacher's reputation is based solely on the success of her students—and successful they are! Ms. Miller has students receiving standing ovations on Broadway, pleasing crowds at Walt Disney World in Orlando and Tokyo Disneyland in Japan, bringing Christmas joy to Radio City Music Hall, and wowing visitors in Las Vegas—many have performed all over the world. For every child who has gone on to dance professionally, there are a hundred more who have traveled to exciting cities, stayed in four-star hotels, and won major competitions. Thanks to Ms. Miller, there are countless more who have stood a little taller, spoken a little louder, and learned the value of hard work. She truly teaches a child that *everything is possible*!

Ms. Miller gained international recognition for her hit TV series *Dance Moms,* the highest-rated show on the Lifetime network, and debuted her newest project on Lifetime, *Abby's Ultimate Dance Competition*. She has received accolades from around the world, inspiring countless children to dance. As *Dance Moms* hits Season 4.5 and its one hundredth episode, Ms. Miller has been offered another show with her family at Lifetime. Ms. Miller also owns two retail stores: Broadway Baby's Dancewear and Costume Shoppe, located adjacent to the dance studio in Pittsburgh, and another in the downtown area. All Abby Lee Apparel is available online.